THE QUESTION OF THE OTHER

Tang Chun-I Lecture Series

The Tang Chun-I Lecture Series is based on lectures and seminars delivered by distinguished scholars who are holding the Tang Chun-I Visiting Professorship at The Chinese University of Hong Kong. This professorship was initiated in 2003 by the Department of Philosophy, The Chinese University of Hong Kong, in memory of the late Professor Tang Chun-I (1909–1978), a major figure in twentieth-century Chinese philosophy and the first Chair Professor of the Department of Philosophy.

The Question of the Other

Bernhard Waldenfels

The Tang Chun-I Lecture for 2004

The Chinese University Press

State University of New York Press

ISBN: The Chinese University Press 978-962-996-277-7
ISBN: State University of New York Press 978-0-7914-7371-9 (hc)—978-0-7914-7372-6 (pb)

Published for North America by:
State University of New York Press
Albany, New York
www.sunypress.edu

Production by Ryan Morris
Marketing by Fran Keneston

Published for the rest of the world by:
The Chinese University Presss
The Chinese University of Hong Kong
Sha Tin, N.T., Hong Kong
Fax: +852 2603 6692
+852 2603 7355
E-mail: cup@cuhk.edu.hk
Web site: www.chineseupress.com

Printed in the United States of America

Library of Congress Cataloging-in-Publication Data

Waldenfels, Bernhard, 1934–
The question of the other / Berhard Waldenfels.
p. cm.
Includes bibliographical references.
ISBN 978-0-7914-7371-9 (hardcover : alk. paper) | 978-0-7914-7372-6 (pbk. : alk. paper)
ISBN 978-0-7914-7859-2 (e-book)

1. Other (Philosophy) I. Title.
128'.4—dc22

2007016671

10 9 8 7 6 5 4 3 2 1

Contents

Preface

The Chinese University of Hong Kong seems to be a good place to question the Otherness of other people and other cultures, including one's own otherness. This university belongs to a city which is not only a harbour city, but also bears the harbour in its name, and which for a long time has been a door to the West, preferring the ruse of money to the violence of weapons. But as its name indicates, the university is also rooted in the ancient culture of China whose history of dynasties and empires over thousands of years makes Old Europe look rather young. Take the reign of signs. The picture elements of Chinese word signs are not simply banished into the prehistory of writing. Like everything which has been invented these linguistic signs go back to trial stages, the traces of which are preserved on bones and bronze, but to a certain extent at least some are used — so to speak — as they were on the second or third day of their invention. We Europeans are astonished to learn that the Chinese and Japanese use more or less the same characters, although they write them each in their own particular way. That looks like an Eastern Pentecost, at least on a certain level, as if everyone hears the other speak in his or her own language.[1] We encounter here a special kind of universality, located not before and/or beyond the letter, but realised through the letter, or to put it more precisely, through ideograms which to some extent *show* what they *say*. Not least by virtue of reference to their common Greek and Latin heritage, European languages also have much in common, but when Germans do not understand what French people are saying it does not help very much to write it down. Thus we are translators through and through, apart from some bodily gestures which in general do not need an interpreter. There is nothing like a single European language. Europe is multilingual and it will remain so, as long as we refuse to speak, to think or to love exclusively in English.

Yet before I start to poach on intercultural territories let me turn to the land I will try to till in my lectures. In my mother tongue I would present the question I am going to pursue as the *Frage nach dem Fremden.* But what does that precisely mean? Are we going to question the foreigner, the stranger, the strange, the alien or simply the Other? And if we are asking about the Other, do we refer only to other persons or also to other things, and should we not make a distinction between he-other and she-other? The German language (which, as we know, is not only spoken by Germans) forces us to decide whether we want to speak of *der, die* or *das Fremde.* From the very beginning the Other appears as a gendered Other, even if we generally try to neglect this. But on the other hand, the German language allows us to postpone, at least for a while, the sort of word splitting which other languages have to do when they speak of *Fremdes.* I am inclined to imitate Gertrude Stein by saying: *Fremdes ist Fremdes ist Fremdes.* Or let me invoke as an ally the famous Austrian composer: "*Fremd bin ich eingezogen, / fremd zieh ich wieder aus,*" which in English could sound roughly like this: "As a stranger I arrived, / as a stranger I leave again." Does this mean that Schubert is speaking and singing only of the *stranger* when he evokes the *Fremdheit* of this winter traveller? And do we really understand the German word when we simply translate it in this or in that way? It seems to me that the *Fremde* is one of those cultural key-words which, though not untranslatable, are ultimately over-determined through translation when, like our dreams, they touch on the *Unheimliche,* the uncanny. Doing philosophy means awakening, but perhaps we should not awake in such a way that we forget the "stuff of dreams" and, together with it, the "*Stoff des Fremden.*"

* * *

But before transforming the pre-face into the face itself I shall come to a stop again. For the reader, who follows the footsteps of those who attended the lectures, it may be sufficient to know what he or she has to expect. Lecture I and Lecture II will go straight to the central topic of otherness or alienness, surveying the historical and linguistic surroundings, sketching different dimensions of alienness and fighting against a certain personal and collective *horror alieni* i.e. against being horrified by what is alien and treating what is alien as horrible. We must concede that even philosophers are often affected and infected by this sort of horror. My own reflections are born from the following assumptions. The alien occurs and affects us by way of a sort of *pathos* which precedes, provokes and requires our *response.* Both pathos and response cross each other without converging, they are separated from each other by a hiatus which I call *diastasis.* This means that every sort of appropriation comes too late to overcome the alien which haunts us. In Lectures III and IV these central assumptions will be further elaborated by exploring the event character and the time aspect which shape our experience of the alien. Lectures V, VI and VII turn to important issues such as corporeality, violence and place. Each of them opens up specific horizons of alienness or otherness, but remain far from exhaustive. Horizons are nothing more than borderlines of seeing, moving, acting and speaking, pointing to an inexhaustible beyond. Each of the following lectures will be preceded by an opening or overture which gives a certain taste of what is going to be treated by means of concepts. This may make it easier to keep in mind the *surplus* — everything that appears exceeds what is said about it. Relatively frequent references to corresponding disciplines which are inserted into the train of thought take account of the strange situation philosophers are exposed to. They may have good reasons to behave like lonely hunters sometimes, but nevertheless they do not have a monopoly on the things they are dealing with. The famous "things themselves" are situated at the cross-roads of various disciplines and practices, and they are accordingly not free of political presuppositions and consequences, as indirect as these may be. In Europe the birth of philosophy, geometry, tragedy and democracy occurred in the same place. This may have been due to a special cultural constellation, it certainly also had and has its dark sides; and beyond this, Athens was not the only cultural hub of the universe. Nevertheless, it is difficult to presume that philosophy, whatever one may call it and wherever it may emerge, comes out of the blue.

* * *

Let me mention some last details concerning the actual circumstances and the textual basis of the present lectures. Lectures I, II, V, VII were given as weekly lectures to a student audience, Lectures III and VI were inserted as public lectures, given to the inviting Faculty and to the Philosophical Institute, and Lecture IV has been added as an encore. Some of the texts on which the lectures are based have been published before or simultaneously in a first version. On the occasion of their collective publication they were all reworked and they have been completed with some, let us say, humble findings I was able to make during my stay in Hong Kong. I thank Donald Goodwin for his assistance with the English versions, and I thank Professor Tze-wan Kwan for putting the finishing touches to the whole.

Previous publications

Lecture II: "Antwort auf das Fremde. Grundzüge einer responsiven Phänomenologie." First published in Japanese in *Metaphysica. The Journal of Philosophy and Ethics* (Dep. of Philosophy, Faculty of Letters, Osaka University), No. 27 (1996), pp. 1–15. German Version in B. Waldenfels, I. Därmann, eds., *Der Anspruch des Anderen. Perspektiven phänomenologischer Ethik*, München: W. Fink, 1998. Further translations into Czech, English, French, Hungarian, Polish, Russian and Spanish.

Lecture III: "Die Macht der Ereignisse." In M. Rölli, ed., *Ereignis auf Französisch*, München: W. Fink, 2004, and in *Ästhetik Erfahrung*, Interventionen 13, ed. J. Huber, Institut für Theorie der Gestaltung und Kunst Zürich, Zürich: Ed. Voldemeer/Wien, New York: Springer 2004.

Lecture IV: "Time Lag: Motifs for a Phenomenology of the Experience of Time," trans. D. Calandrella (transl. revised by the author). In *Research in Phenomenology* 30 (2000), pp. 107–119. German version: "Zeitverschiebung." In A. Kablitz, W. Oesterreicher, R. Warning , eds., *Zeit und Text*, München: W. Fink 2003.

Lecture V: "Leibliche Erfahrung zwischen Selbstheit und Andersheit." In U. Bröckling, A. T. Paul, St. Kaufmann, eds., *Vernunft – Entwicklung – Leben*, München: W. Fink 2004. First written in English on the occasion of an opening speech at the "Center for Subjectivity Research" at the University of Copenhagen, given in September 2002: "Bodily Experience between Selfhood and Otherness." In *Phenomenology and Cognitive Science* (forthcoming).

Lecture VI: "Aporien der Gewalt." In M. Dabag, A. Kapust, B. Waldenfels, eds., *Gewalt. Strukturen, Formen, Repräsentationen*, München: W. Fink, 2000.

Concerning the background of the main ideas presented in these lectures, I refer first of all to *Antwortregister* (1994) and *Bruchlinien der Erfahrung* (2002) where the conception of a responsive and pathos-orientated phenomenology is unfolded in full length. The initial ideas leading to the assumption of a radical and genuine alienness are to be found in *Ordnung im Zwielicht* (1987), English: *Order in the Twilight* (1996). Later on the same conception has been tested in different areas such as interculturality, ethnology and politics, epistemology and technology, further *aisthesis* in relation to painting, music and architecture and finally the many voices of speech, close to Bakhtin's polylogue (see *Der Stachel des Fremden*, 1990, and four volumes *Studien zur Phänomenologie des Fremden*, 1997–1999, and it has been recently resumed under the title *Grundmotive einer Phänomenologie des Fremden*, 2006). The common background of our corporeal existence and of our bodily behaviour is unfolded in a series of lectures edited by Regula Giuliani under the title *Das leibliche Selbst* (2000).

* * *

It remains for me to thank all those who made it possible for me to teach as Tang Chun-I Visiting Professor at the Chinese University of Hong Kong. So I thank the Department of Philosophy for inviting me, I thank Gateway Management Services in the name of Mr. Raphael Che for sponsoring the Tang Chun-I Lectures, and also I thank the patient helpers working in the secretary's office of the department who showed me the right way whenever I got lost in the institutional or technical jungle. Finally and above all I thank Professor Tze-wan Kwan, Professor Chan-fai Cheung, Professor Kwok-ying Lau and all their colleagues for receiving me with great hospitality, for giving me some exciting intercultural lectures and for creating — together with their students — such a good atmosphere, allowing us to discuss with and learn from each other — under the sign of what may be called *freundliche Fremdheit.*

Bochum, June 2004

Left: Prof. Bernhard Waldenfels (Professor Emeritus, Ruhr-Universität Bochum, Germany); *Right*: Prof. Tze-wan Kwan (Formerly Chairman, Department of Philosophy, CUHK).

From Left to Right: Ping-keung Lui (PolyU), Kwok-keung Lau (CUHK), Robert Davies, Stephen Palmquist (HKBU), Mei-yee Leung (CUHK), Christopher Fraser (CUHK), Xiaogan Liu (CUHK), Yuen-sang Leung (CUHK), Chan-fai Cheung (CUHK), Bernhard Waldenfels (Ruhr-Universität Bochum), Tze-wan Kwan (CUHK), Kwok-ying Lau (CUHK), Chad Hansen (HKU), Gerhold Becker (HKBU), Qingjie Wang (CUHK), Brigitta Blaha-Silva (Austrian Consulate General, Hong Kong), Jürgen Keil (Goethe Institute Hong Kong).

Lecture I

Experience of the Other

Opening: *Picture magic.* — In his famous studies of religious rituals, which were published in 1931 under the title *The Golden Bough*, James George Frazer denounces the magic use of pictures in such a way that all kinds of otherness lapse into a sea of superstition. Wittgenstein's remarks on Frazer are no less famous.[1] He writes: "Burning in effigy. Kissing the picture of one's beloved. That is *obviously not* based on the belief that it will have some specific effect on the object which the picture represents. It aims at satisfaction and achieves it. Or rather: it *aims* at nothing at all; we just behave this way and then we feel satisfied. One could also kiss the name of one's beloved, and here it would be clear that the name was being used as a substitute." In order to dissipate the suspicion that the savage may live in a pure fantasy world he notes: "The same savage, who stabs the picture of his enemy apparently in order to kill him, really builds his hut and carves his arrow skilfully and not in effigy." The tenor of Wittgenstein's critique is as follows: things become incomprehensible, senseless, irrational if we confuse the symbolic effects on life with real effects on nature, yielding to certain prejudices we have inherited. "What a narrow spiritual life on Frazer's part! As a result: how impossible it was for him to conceive a life different from that of the England of his time!" Through these remarks runs a common thread, leading from strange things through our practice of the strange to ethnology as a special kind of research dealing with what appears as culturally strange or alien. In all these cases we are faced with the problem of how to face otherness or alienness without taking away its sting.

* * *

The Rise of the Alien in Western History

The rise of the alien resembles the sunrise. Just like the sun it appears suddenly. At the same time it does not resemble it because, unlike the sun, whose rising we are accustomed to, the alien surprises us. It goes beyond our expectations, it is not easy to grasp, it enters unsummoned. But precisely in this odd way it does belong to our everyday life, appearing as something unfamiliar within the familiar. First, there is the law of hospitality which, applicable to strangers or foreigners in this or in that way, belongs to the basic elements of every culture. In our Western culture, the Hebraic tradition of the Bible demands a special respect for the status of the alien. The Greeks, who conferred on Zeus the epithet Ζεῦς ξένιος, i.e. the God of aliens or of guests, had numerous legal prescriptions governing the special status of all those who were not full citizens of the town.[2] Islamic culture, arising on the borders of deserts where travellers are more in need of the assistance of others than elsewhere, regulated the coming and going of guests in its own way. Guests may stay for three days and during this time everything is at their disposal. After that they either become integrated or they have to leave. Apart from the realm of hospitality, there is the common phenomenon of the foreign language, the *Fremdsprache.* In German we have some special expressions centred on the alien. Let me mention the behaviour of the baby, which as a rule at the age of about four months learns to discriminate between the familiar face of the mother or a motherly person to which it responds and unfamiliar faces from which it turns away. In German we call this discriminating behaviour *Fremdeln.*[3] Further, there is the clinical phenomenon of alienation or *Entfremdung,* which gained an important socio-pathological significance in the writings of Karl Marx. Finally, there is the artistic method of alienation or *Verfremdung,* which Bertold Brecht made famous in the art of theatre. He learned about it from the method of *ostranenie,* introduced by the Russian formalists who for their part referred back to Aristotle. In Aristotle's *Rhetoric* (see III, 2–3) unusual expressions are characterised as alien (ξένον or ξενικόν). For us Germans, the poetry and the music of the Romantics is full of motifs touching on the alien. Take only Schubert's *Winter Journey*: "*Fremd bin ich eingezogen, / fremd zieh ich wieder aus,*" "As a stranger I arrived, / as a stranger I leave again." I am quite certain that in Eastern traditions one could see the continuation of this theme in one way or another.

But if we turn to the great Western philosophers the scene changes. By no means does the phenomenon of the alien belong to the fundamental equipment of occidental thought. For centuries we find only what I call a *relative* kind of alienness, dependent on a limited standpoint or on early phases of development. We do not find a radical kind of alienness which goes down to the root of things and cannot be derived from anything else. In Aristotelian terms: only an alien *for us* is accepted, but not an alien *in itself*. Take the overwhelming vision of the cosmos. The cosmic order encompasses everything and everybody. The cosmos is like a great house (*oikos*) overcoming the distinction between the own and the alien: after all, it is our house and we inhabit it jointly. In this way the phenomenon of the alien is domesticated, which literally means: adapted to and integrated into one's own house or home.[4] Thus the Greek words used for the alien, i.e. ξένον or ἀλλοῖον, are far from being key terms. At best we find some important, but rather eccentric, figures who are apostrophised as strange(r) (ξένος or ξένη): Diotima in the *Symposium*, the stranger from Elea in the *Sophist*, or Socrates himself at the beginning of the *Apology*.[5] Generally speaking, all human beings have the same *logos* as their common logos (κοινὸς λόγος), and the more rational we are, the less alien we are to each other. However that is only half of the truth. In the 5th century B.C. the difference between Greeks and barbarians emerges. This distinction did not yet exist in Homer's epics, written in the 8th century, which came to be as canonical in Greek culture and education as the Bible or the texts of Confucius did elsewhere. In the *Iliad* Hector, fighting on the Trojan side, is not at all inferior to Achilles, the great hero on the Greek side. The barbarians, so called because they stammer incomprehensible words, are indeed alien, not on the horizontal axis as other people but on the vertical axis as inferior people. It is interesting to see that the difference between being reasonable and being barbarian arises at the same time as a strict monopolisation of the logos took place and the fratricidal war *among* Greeks was clearly distinguished from the war of extermination *against* barbarians (see Plato's *Republic* 470 b–c).[6] The following centuries in Europe had their own barbarians in terms of savages,[7] pagans, Huns, Turks, Gypsies, *vaterlandslose Gesellen*,[8] enemies of the people, *Untermenschen* and so on. Traditions are not always edifying.

The situation we have outlined begins to change with the modern era, although this change is charged with all sorts of hesitation, delay and compromise, persisting until today. The fact that the phenomenon of the alien has finally crossed the threshold of problematization goes back to a double mutation in Western culture, a mutation in modern *rationality* on the one hand and in the role of the modern *subject* on the other hand. Reason as an all-encompassing order and the subject as the central figure are the two points of attack. Apart from that, the two maintain a strained relation with each other: reason stands for what we have in common, whereas subjectivity has at least in part to do with what belongs to me as an individual. In any case, radical alienness enters the scene only under the condition that alienness reaches the core of Being and the heart of the self. Consequently, reason or order dissipate, and the subject becomes decentred. This process has the effect that human beings will never be completely at home in the world, and that nobody can claim to be the master of his own home. There are some early signs of change, such as the Hegelian-Marxian concept of *Entfremdung*, i.e. alienation. Nevertheless, *passing through the alien* is not the same as *being provoked by the alien*. The philosophy of *Entfremdung* only flirts with the possibility of *Fremdheit*. The undermining ideas of Kierkegaard and Nietzsche are more radical. But it is only in the 20th century that the question of alienness or otherness becomes a central philosophical issue, sketched by Simmel, Benjamin, Adorno and Bloch, systematically elaborated by Husserl, finally radicalised by French phenomenologists and by those who make common cause with them. Thus the motive of alienness or otherness has become a sort of touchstone for what I call the *Verfremdung der Moderne*, i.e. a process through which modernity discovers its own fissures and abysses.[9]

Linguistic and Conceptual Shades

The alien emerges as a peculiar phenomenon which does not simply yield to the general logos of the phenomena. Linguistic observations and conceptual analyses show clearly enough that the alien is a highly complex phenomenon. In German we have the one word *fremd* which contains different shades of meaning without disintegrating into pure homonyms. In the well-known classical and modern languages of the Western world the word *fremd* has to be translated by different words, dependent on the shade of meaning involved.

Fremd means first that which lies *outside of one's own domain* (see ξένον *externum, foreign, stranger, étranger*).[10] As far as I can see, the Chinese word *wài*, connecting being alien with being outside, fits into this line. The contrast between inside and outside returns on the social level in terms of insiders and outsiders, of in-groups and out-groups. One could also mention the *peregrine*, derived from the Latin word *peregrinus*, which literally means "roaming through the fields (*per agros*)." This is also what the *Landstreicher* i.e. the tramp does, or the medieval *pilgrim*. In Latin a foreign word is called *vox peregrina* – *Wort aus der Fremde*.[11] From the world of music we know the *Peregrina-Lieder*, composed by Hugo Wolf. They go back to a series of poems which the Swabian poet Eduard Mörike, fully bewildered and embarrassed, wrote about a foreign girl, a *Mädchen aus der Fremde*. As we can see, being outside or coming from the outside is not only an issue for police stations and immigration offices, although it is never free from political connotations.

The word *fremd* means secondly everything *which belongs to others* (see ἀλλότριον, *alienum, alien, ajeno*). This second meaning opens a field of questions that is no smaller than the previous one, revolving around problems like having something, taking into possession, being the individual or collective owner of property. The dimension of having, which stands in contrast with the dimensions of being or doing, is deeply rooted in our bodily dispositions. Being at hand presupposes hands which grasp and seize, sometimes clinging to what they touch. But the states of having are also embedded in institutions of property. They are based on economics, politics and law, and they are interrupted by gestures of giving which pass beyond the symmetry of exchange. The concrete forms of possession and ownership find their echo in general ontological features. The *property* somebody has acquired is extended to qualities, ascribed to persons as well as to things. Whereas the Latin root word *proprietas* is related to *propre* (= near by), which has a local basis, in German *Eigentum, Eigentümlichkeit* and even *Eigentlichkeit* are more directly connected with a process of *Aneignung* (appropriation). The process of appropriation reaches in Hegel the heights of the Spirit, passing through all kinds of otherness, but ultimately returning to itself, thanks to the cunning of dialectic reason. We will later see to what extent the experience of Otherness is overshadowed by attempts of appropriation.

But *fremd* has yet another meaning. It means, thirdly, that *which strikes us as heterogeneous*, as *fremdartig* (see ξένον, *strange, étrange*). This last shade of alienness evokes in particular the very experience by which something appears as alien, breaking up the "community of genera," the κοινωνία τῶν γενῶν (see Plato's *Sophist* 250 d ff.), evoking "another genus" and generating feelings of astonishment, of perplexity, of bewilderment, of anxiety. Philosophers would be more attentive to the phenomenon of the alien if they took astonishment or wonder not merely as the first step towards wisdom or knowledge, but as the initiation into "another state" (Musil) that we will never leave behind. At this point philosophy crosses paths with ethnology as a specific science of the alien, which has, however, its own burdens.

The Same, the Self and the Ambiguity of Otherness

To begin we have distinguished between three aspects of alienness which can be summarized as the aspects of *place, property,* and *manner.* Now it seems that these different aspects do not have the same weight. The first appears to be decisive, not only in order to grasp the phenomenon as a whole, but also in order to discover the radicalness of the alienness we have in mind.

This pre-eminence becomes obvious as soon as we confront the special phenomenon of the *alien* with the category of the *other,* one of the most traditional forms of ontology. What we encounter as alien is not simply something other or different. If we continue using one and the same term, speaking in both cases of "the other" or of "l'autre," as the French do,[12] the term otherness becomes ambiguous. Without trying to prescribe a general use of language, I myself prefer to cultivate a difference between *Andersheit* and *Fremdheit,* which is quite common in German[13] but not in English. Therefore I shall frequently use the more current term "otherness" when speaking of alienness, but in any case it should be clear what we are speaking about. Otherwise all our reflections will become confused or, even worse, they will lead back to the philosophical shortcomings we want to overcome.

The difference between the two forms of otherness comes out clearly when we consider what the opposite to each type of otherness is and how the two oppositions are formed. As we will see, the genealogy and, at the same time, the topology of alienness differs considerably from that of simple otherness. Otherness, first analysed in Plato's *Sophist*, comes about through a process of delimitation (*Abgrenzung*) which opposes the *same* (ταὐτόν, *idem*) to the other (ἕτερον, *aliud*). When distinguishing between apple and pear, between table and bed, nobody would claim that the one is alien or foreign to the other. The one is simply different from the other, it is what the other is not. The relational proposition "A is not B" can always be reversed to yield "B is not A." From the viewpoint of a "third" party who draws the distinction, both sides are at the same distance, just as in the case of the judge or the arbitrator who makes a neutral decision, standing above the parties involved. The alien, in contrast, does not arise from a mere process of delimitation. It emerges from a process which is realised simultaneously as an inclusion (*Eingrenzung*) and an exclusion (*Ausgrenzung*). The alien is not opposed to the same, rather it refers to the *Self* (αὐτός, *ipse*), to myself or to ourselves, including the "sphere of ownness" (see Hua I, § 44) from which it escapes. What is alien does not simply appear different, rather it arises from elsewhere. The sphere of alienness is separated from my sphere of ownness by a threshold, as is the case for sleep and wakefulness, health and sickness, age and youth, and no one ever stands on both sides of the threshold at the same time. This also holds true for the difference between human beings and animals or for the difference between genders and between cultures. There is no "third man" necessary to differentiate the male from the female, since male beings distinguish *themselves* from female beings, and similarly female beings from male beings. Nor is there a cultural arbitrator to divide European and Far Eastern cultures from the outside, since Europeans must have distinguished *themselves* from Asians before such a division or comparison can be made.

Moreover there are many historically and culturally diverse ways of distinguishing oneself from the other. As far as the Western world is concerned, we have already mentioned the rather aggressive exclusion of the so-called barbarians and their followers, and we have pointed out the fact that the Greek manner of seeing things in black and white occurs rather late, due to a certain monopolisation of the "logos." The isolation of Japanese culture from all foreign influence, which lasted for two centuries up until the modernisation efforts during the Meiji period, belongs on a completely different page of history. On yet another page appears life under Turkish rule in the south-east part of Europe, something that has had an effect up until the recent war in the Balkans. There is no "alien" as such, there are rather different styles of alienness or otherness. Otherness has an occasional character. As Husserl would say, it is relative to changing standpoints. A placeless "alien in general" would resemble a "left side in general" — a monstrous idea, confusing place indications with conceptual determinations.

We may conclude that the distinction between the Self and the Other, between ownness and alienness, cannot be reduced to two *terms.* Rather it refers to two different *topoi.* The experience of the Other cannot be included in any ontology whatsoever, as an ontology would subordinate Where-questions to What-questions; on the contrary, it requires a new kind of topology or, when we include the descriptive part, a new kind of topography.

Alienness as Incarnate Absence

Moreover, the alien's place is a peculiar place. It resists any attempt to insert it into a local grid which would be accessible to everyone; it can only be reached by crossing a certain threshold. It was Husserl who put the question of the otherness of the Other in a new and radical way, and who at once gave it a paradoxical turn. In his *Cartesian Meditations,* which go back to his Sorbonne Lectures of 1929, he characterises the experience of the Other as the "verifiable accessibility of what is originally inaccessible" (Hua I, 144, Engl. 114). This definition shows some remarkable aspects.

First, the alien is not defined by what it *is.* An ontological kind of question would presuppose that the alien is embedded in some essential structure that can be known in advance. Nor is the question of the other reduced to the question of how to know it. To ask how we gain knowledge of the other would still presuppose too much, namely a pure fact we know or do not know. On the contrary, to define the alien by way of its accessibility means that the path of approach pertains to its very being. It is what it is in appearing in this or that way. In other words, we are confronted with a phenomenology of the other whose *logos* is drawn from the phenomenon itself.

Secondly, the paradoxical definition, which combines possibility and impossibility in a peculiar way, points to the fact that alienness has nothing to do with mere lack or deficiency — as if the alien were something not yet or no longer known, but waiting to be known. On the contrary, absence, distance or inaccessibility constitute alienness or otherness as such.[14] In this regard the phenomenon of alienness resembles the past which cannot be grasped in any other way than by its after-effects or by recollection. The alien does not simply dwell elsewhere, it reveals itself as an "original of the elsewhere" (Merleau-Ponty 1964b, p. 308, Engl. p. 254), as a form of *atopia*, quite in line with Plato who in his *Symposium* uses Alcibiades' voice to describe Socrates as an *atopos* — as somebody strange and placeless. Whoever or whatever appears as alien is never completely in place.

We shall now enter into different dimensions of the alien, each of them leading to specific problems which will be further deepened in the following lectures.

My Own and the Other's Alienness

First, the alien does not simply emerge outside of myself, it already appears within myself and within ourselves in terms of an intra-subjective and intra-cultural otherness. There is not just another or a second I, an *alter ego*, but rather, as Rimbaud puts it, we must concede: "I is another" (*Je est un autre*). The *I* is not a superior person who, at least for a certain time, presides and governs speech, holding the title of the speaking subject. From the very beginning of speech I speak and am spoken to at once, exactly as indicated by the agrammatical twist of Rimbaud's saying.[15] Let us give some examples. As a being that is born I find myself living in a world that I did not create. I bear names that I received from others, primarily the "first name," the "given name" or *Rufname* (in Chinese: *ming* or *naiming* = literally milk name) which we directly owe to others, secondly the "surname"or "family name" (in Chinese *xing*) which has its origin in the chain of generations; and as we know the series of name-giving does not stop there. Further, I discover myself by and in the Other's eyes as I do in the looking-glass, which is, so to speak, a glass looking back at me. In this way I find myself marked by a chasm which prevents the person who says *I* or *je* from coinciding with the spoken *me* or *moi*. Descartes could have discovered this if he had paid more attention to the saying of the *cogito* and not only to being and knowing it. The contextuality of the *I*, which is never fully individualised and always bears features of a nameless no one (Merleau-Ponty 1964b, p. 299, Engl. p. 246), comes to light better in languages like Japanese where personal pronouns show a greater variability than in our Western languages and where sentences are less personalised. Our languages are much more person-centred and so it is hard to find equivalents for such a Japanese sequence as: *nani shiteruno* (literally: "What doing?") — *ongaku o kiiterundayo* (literally: "Listening to music"). Things are similar in Chinese, where we find sentences such as *bu gan* (literally: "not dare"), which leaves it open who at what time and in what way does not dare. The German Sinologist Georg von der Gabelentz, from whose Chinese Grammar (1960, p. 118) I take this example, explicitly warns against personalising something which displays impersonal features, and Nietzsche also mocks our mania for assuming that wherever there is a deed there must be a doer (*Jenseits von Gut und Böse*, aph. 17, KSA, vol. 5, p. 31). But is it really the case that in such cases we are always confronted with a deed, as the grammatical form of the active verbs suggests? When Lichtenberg advises us to say "it thinks" (*es denkt*) as we say in German "it is lightning" (*es blitzt*) and when other writers heed this advice (see below p. 43), they question the overly simple assumption that everything occurring *to me* is caused *by me* — as if we were the master of every idea that comes into our minds. Otherness originates in ourselves; it comes upon us at home. I call this dimension of alienness *ecstatic alienness*, referring to the fact that somebody is or gets outside of himself. This reminds us of Plato's *Phaedrus* (249 c) where the *mania* of *eros* is presented as a sort of ecstasy: the lover steps out the customs of his ordinary life. One may also mention the motive of "ecstasis," related to Heidegger's concept of "ec-sistence" (see Kwan 1995, p. 269 f.), but it makes a considerable difference whether this sort of "out-boundness" (ibid.) remains within the hermeneutic circle circumscribing my own possibilities, or whether it goes back to an experience of the alien which starts from elsewhere.

This may be illustrated by a famous haiku written by the itinerant Japanese poet Basho: "Living in Kyoto / at the call of the cuckoo / I long for Kyoto." The call of the bird may be very familiar, nevertheless it can startle us out of what is common or ordinary. It may do this time after time, as long as we are ready to be surprised, listening to the echo of absent sounds or voices in what is present. Or to quote from Goethe's *West-Eastern Divan,* one of the rare examples of explicitly intercultural borderline poetry: "Unmöglich scheint immer die Rose, unbegreiflich die Nachtigall" i.e. "The rose always seems impossible, the nightingale inconceivable." Someone who disregards his or her own otherness finds only the same things and the same self everywhere, no matter how many countries and seas are crossed.

If we now turn to the alienness of the Other, we find something which seems to be much easier to accept. But what does this really mean? Let us again start with a Cartesian story. In the second of his *Meditations* the philosopher presents himself, sitting in his armchair, thinking and doubting. He imagines the case that hats and clothes pass outside before his window, and he wonders how he can find out whether these are not mere dummies but living people like himself. What is interesting for us is not so much the arguments the philosopher gives, but the sheer assumption that the existence of the Other depends on my judgement, as if I were a policeman before whom others have to prove their identity. What is dubious from the beginning is the basic presumption that my gaze out of the window precedes the Other's gaze from outside the window. This kind of philosophy squares with Alberti's theory of painting which compares the look at the canvas with a look through the window. However assuming that there are others like me who only complement my position in the world, and that they do this in terms of an *alter ego* presupposing my own ego as the *first ego,* is far from all our experience of the Other; it is a mere construct. Provided that I experience the Other in terms of a lived and incarnate absence, I feel myself seen by the Other before I see him or her, I feel myself spoken to before addressing him or her, I feel myself seized by the desire of the Other before seeking him or her. The Other's gaze, voice and desire constitute the very event of becoming visible, audible or desirable, and this event exceeds everything that can be seen, heard or striven for. As Paul suggests, the Other is a sort of double, the shadow of myself, too close to be avoided, too remote to be grasped (see below pp. 47, 76). I call this kind of alienness *duplicative alienness.*

This further kind of alienness is again given poetic expression in Goethe's *Divan.* In his poem *Gingko Biloba* Goethe takes the split leaf of this time-honoured Eastern temple tree as an example of the lover and the poet doubling himself in the Other: "That I am one and two."

Presupposing that we distinguish between the otherness of oneself and that of others, one may ask which comes first. My answer would be: neither of them is first. If I become myself only by being touched by the Other and responding to his or her appeal, the two dimensions intersect: I am outside of myself precisely in being duplicated by the Other, and I am duplicated precisely in getting outside of myself. More about this will be said in the following lectures on responsivity and our bodily experience.

Alienness Outside Order and Below Order

A further dimension of alienness arises from the web or network of order. By order we mean certain dispositions of things, corresponding to certain connections of ideas, both subject to certain rules. The Greeks called order *cosmos,* which has a connotation of beauty, or *taxis* which has a military connotation, referring to the formation of troops on the battlefield. The meaning of order still remains double-edged, oscillating between disposition and command. The German word *Anordnung* means both. But for classical Greeks such as Plato and Aristotle order was mainly rooted in the nature of things, not unlike the ideas of Confucian ethics. Greek cosmology was integrated into the Jewish-Christian vision of a created order by Augustine, the author of a book specifically on order (*De ordine*), with the result that the order of things was now sustained by divine commands. In contrast the modern concept of order, which emerged at the time of Descartes and Hobbes, is deeply marked by contingency. Things are what they are, human beings are who they are, but the course of things and human affairs could be to some extent different. Assuming that there is more that is possible than what actually becomes real does not mean that everything is possible. Ulrich, the protagonist of Musil's *Man without Qualities,* puts this in theological terms. He gives Leibniz a slap, presuming that God would prefer to speak of his world in the *conjunctivus potentialis*: "God makes the world, thinking it could just as well be different" (1978,

p. 19). This combination of creativity and contingency finds a distant echo in the motto which the Chinese painter Liu Guo Song uses, struggling with a certain traditionalism for which "learning is like building a pyramid." The motto is: "To be different before being good."[16] Or should we say: "To be different in being good"? In any case, what is at stake here can be put quite well in phenomenological terms: something appears *as something, as somebody,* but in such a way that it appears in this way *rather than in another.* This "rather"[17] has to be connected with something like a principle of insufficient reason, because every order which could be other than it is turns out to be selective and exclusive. As Nietzsche points out, every process of ordering can be characterised as a process of "equalising what is not equal."[18] The surplus of otherness or of heterogeneity which exceeds the given order may be called *extraordinary alienness.*

But alienness is not only to be encountered beyond the given order as its other side, we also find it on this side of order. Whatever or whoever is *put in order* without previously *being in order*[19] crosses a threshold, once emerging and then sinking back. This happens in processes such as awakening and falling asleep or being born and dying, which always have something uncanny about them.[20] Such threshold experiences, traditionally accompanied by specific rituals of passage, pertain to the pathetic background of our experience. The type of alienness which characterises these infra-ordinal experiences, which all take place either on this side or on the other side of a threshold, may be called *liminal alienness.* This sort of alienness is represented by mythical images such as *chaos* (i.e. the yawning abyss), *tohubohu* (i.e. confusion, pêle-mêle, *Durcheinander*) or the *raw* or *rude* (i.e. the unformed). Instead of remaining caught in the alternative of either rationalising the sphere of myth or leaving it to pure esoteric trends, we should direct our attention to the zones of the chaotic which constitute the margins of and the holes in our ordinary life. Even Husserl, whom nobody would suspect of being an irrationalist, takes disorder (*Unordnung*) as a primary phenomenon (*Urphänomen*) (Hua XI, 134) i.e. not as the negation of order but as its birth-place. There are many motifs such as the abyss of freedom, evoked by Schelling, Kiekegaard and Heidegger; the nightly confusion of our dreams, interpreted by Freud as a mighty imagery; the positive indeterminacy of the open horizons of our experience, explored by Husserl; the vague experience which has found its proper elaboration in terms of a Fuzzy Logic, or chaos theory, which relies on incalculable shifts that interrupt our calculations.[21] Both limit-states, the one preceding order and the other exceeding it, touch each other, with the effect that extraordinary alienness has its infra-ordinary roots. The path from the *mythos* to the *logos* cannot be reversed, but there are cross-roads and transfer-points through which alienness continues to invade reason and order.

Ways of Appropriation

It would be a great illusion to expect that one day otherness or alienness will bloom like a thousand flowers. Throughout the course of our history we have come across a resistance to alienness, and this resistance does indeed have certain features in common with the type of resistance that psychoanalysis struggles with. The experience of the Other largely coincides with the history of its appropriation. It has often been claimed that Western thought and practice has to be characterised as an attempt to appropriate and dominate the world. Thus, at the beginning of the modern era Descartes proclaims in his *Discours* (AT VI, 62) that human beings should become "masters and owners of nature," and this inevitably includes the mastering of others and of ourselves. Similarly, according to Locke, it is labour that gives a "right of property," extending from one's own person to the work of our hands and changing nature from a "common mother" into a supplier of "the almost worthless materials" (*The Second Treatise of Government,* V).

The process of appropriation is based on what C. B. Macpherson (1962) has called "possessive individualism." This involves the atomisation of the world into individuals, and from everyone's struggle for self-preservation arises a strong barrier between the spheres of ownness and alienness. Now appropriation is realised by different forms of centrism. First there is a kind of *egocentrism* that reduces the alien to the own. The other appears as my double (*alter ego*), as a variation or extension of the own. The well-known method of empathy presupposes that I have something of my own that I can put into the other's soul or mind. This sort of egocentrism, centred on the ego and its own sphere, is complemented by a *logocentrism* centred on the logos as a set of common goals or rules, reducing the alien to the common. In this respect the own and the alien are nothing more than parts of a whole or cases of a rule. Subjectivity is overcome by transsubjectivity, which leaves no real room for intersubjectivity. *Ethnocentrism*, centred on the "we" of one's own group, tribe, nation or culture, can be taken as a collective form of egocentrism, but in its specific forms, especially in the form of *eurocentrism*, it should be interpreted as a mixture of ego- and logocentrism.[22] When we refer to Europe, we often do so in a particular way, for we do not consider and defend it as one culture among others, which would be completely legitimate, but as the incarnation or vanguard of mankind. What does not fit into the scheme of great Reason, true Faith or real Progress is marginalised or, ultimately, eliminated. Thus the figures of the wild, the child, the fool, or the animal are heterogeneous figures, populating the borderlines of an all-encompassing or all-regulating reason. The history of crusades, of colonisation and missions could not have been what it was, namely a mixture of ignorance, curiosity, arrogance and good will, without such a fixed idea propagating the theme of the appropriation of the world.

At present, there are many signs indicating that this process of appropriation, so typical of our Western civilisation, has come to a dead-end. Egocentrism has been increasingly undermined by a *decentring* of the individual and the collective ego. I shall never be able to say in a complete way what or who I am. There are always voices behind me of which I cannot take possession. The place from which I speak is always displaced; I am here and elsewhere, and that means there is no simple centre of speech. Similar things could be said about any attempt to feel completely at home in one's own tribe or nation. Recent forms of nationalism or tribalism are, at best, to be interpreted as filling up a vacuum of sense or as an inappropriate reaction against various forms of over-universalism. With regard to the process of logocentrism, according to Foucault and others we are confronted with a *dispersion* of reason. Reason is dissipated into rationalities, into forms and into worlds of life, which are not subject to one and the same standard and paradigm. There are heterogeneous and incompatible orders that cannot be realised simultaneously.

Does this mean that we are left with nothing but differences and pluralities? If this were true we would stagger from one extreme into the other. But considering the fact that the own is what it is only in contrast to the alien, we become aware that both originate from one and the same process of *differentiation*. In the social field, this process takes different forms and reaches different levels. In Husserl's words we can speak of an *Ineinander*: an *inside each other*, and in the words of the German sociologist Norbert Elias or Merleau-Ponty we may speak of a *Geflecht* and of an *entrelacs* or *entrelacement*: an *intertwining* of the own and the alien.[23] All that leaves behind any form of ontological or sociological atomism. Atomism may be the result of social processes of over-individualisation, but it is will never be the starting point. But instead of going into the details of a general theory of social order, I prefer to take a look at the work of those people whose task it is to come to terms with the alien: I mean the ethnologists.

The Paradox of Xenology

Let us go back to an earlier step of our reflections. If it is true that experience of the other means "accessibility of what is originally inaccessible," how can we make it accessible without diminishing and abolishing its alienness? To claim that every appropriation is limited because of the open horizons of experience and understanding will not suffice to break or stop the process of appropriation. Even in this case the alien would be only relatively alien, as something which has not yet been given or understood, but is awaiting givenness or understanding. Phenomenological experience and hermeneutic understanding, although each directed towards the other, remain ambiguous as long as they cling to a logos encompassing both — the own and the alien.

Ethnology as an empirical science is confronted with this problem in an even sharper sense. If every science consists in determining what is undetermined, in explaining and understanding what cannot be explained or understood, then ethnology as the science of the alien would be a science that tends towards its own abolishment. The more it succeeded, the more it would cancel itself, losing itself by losing its object. This is so because a determined, explained or understood alien would cease to be alien. The alien would vanish. This is what I call the paradox of a science of the alien.

The dilemma of science working against its own project may be the reason why, since Rousseau's days, ethnology has been accompanied by a certain uneasiness or even by a sort of guilty conscience. The dilemma is part of every kind of ethnology that preserves its philosophical impulse, questioning the other or the alien rather than only collecting strange and exotic things. It is not surprising to see that a certain shift has taken place recently within the field of ethnology.[24] This can be clearly shown by considering a certain tension within the work of Lévi-Strauss, the most important ethnologist of our time.

In Lévi-Strauss' work we find two contrasting trends. On the one hand ethnology is practised as a *science of the universal* in terms of *transcultural* structures and codes, reducing the alien to a preliminary form of alienness which, in the long run, will turn out to be a pure variant of invariant rules and structures. But on the other hand, ethnology retains the paradoxical form of a *science of the alien* based on the experience of the other, and understanding the alien as an *intercultural* phenomenon that changes from epoch to epoch, from region to region. Thus Lévi-Strauss characterises ethnology by a movement of *détachement* and *dépaysement*, which comes close to the phenomenological *epoché*, inhibiting the presumptions of one's own culture (see *Structural Anthropology* II, ch. 2). In the same context he quotes from Rousseau's *Essay on the Origin of Languages* (1986, p. 260) in which the author writes: "When one proposes to study men, one has to look close by, but in order to study *man* one has to learn to cast one's glance far."[25] The ethnological view allows us to see ourselves from a distance, from outside.

This has as its consequence a *doubling* and *multiplication* of ethnology. As the French ethnologist Marc Augé (1989) remarks, first, ethnology is split into an ethnology of the other (allo-ethnology) and an ethnology of ourselves (auto-ethnology). But the latter can once again be multiplied into an ethnology exercised *by ourselves or by the other*. As Husserl already presumes, "for myself I am also a stranger for those who are strangers for me" (Hua XV, 635). Thus we can find ethnological studies of Western culture practised by Chinese or African people, breaking the Western monopoly. There is room for more than just one science of the alien, because the concrete forms of alienness differ from each other like the foreignness of foreign languages differs from one language to another. The different forms of ethnology are something like the prolongation of two gazes which cross each other but do not converge. You will never catch sight of me where I see you and vice-versa — I will never catch sight of you where you see me. In a related sense, the science of the alien is an occasional science relative to the standpoint of the investigator in the same way that the so-called occasional expressions such as "I," "you," "here," and "now" refer to the speaker's situation.

But if it is true that the different ways of looking at the other and the different investigations of the other do not converge and do not lead to a universal consensus, how is it possible that we nevertheless have intercourse with each other, living in a common world? How is it possible to understand the other "without sacrificing him to our own logic or our own logic to him"? It is Merleau-Ponty who poses this question in his paper "From Mauss to Lévi-Strauss" (in *Signes* 1960, p. 144). He answers the question by going back to a specific form of ethnological experience that is capable of testing the self through others and others through ourselves. The ethnologist is able to have this experience because there is a "wild region of himself which is not invested in its own culture and by which he communicates with the others" (ibid., p. 151). If we were completely at home in our own culture, the other would remain completely outside of it; there would not be any threshold between our own world and the alien world. A threshold, that is, as a place of passage or transition that we cross but do not surpass in a definitive way.

The same problem was articulated by Lévi-Strauss in one of his last publications. At a conference on the topic of "The place of Japanese culture in the world" held in Kyoto in 1988 (published 1990 in a Japanese journal), Lévi-Strauss starts out from a certain incommensurability of cultures. This leads him to the dilemma that we have no common criteria for judging foreign cultures because either we take them from our own culture, breaching the rules of objectivity, or we take them from the foreign culture, giving up our own standards. Faced with this dilemma, Lévi-Strauss invokes the attraction (and, we should add, the repulsion) of the other culture: the invitation, incitation or appeal to which the ethnologist's look responds and which initiates his research without being integrated into its results. This kind of attraction is the intercultural and also the ethnological phenomenon *par excellence.* Renouncing this phenomenon means renouncing the ethnological experience from which every science of the alien has to start. This science escapes from its self-dissolution only if the alien is more than something not yet known or understood. But what is this "more" that attracts or repels us, what does it mean? What kind of *logos* might be capable of doing justice to it?

Lecture II

Response to the Other

Opening: *Refusal of response.* — In one of his last short stories, entitled *Bartleby the Scrivener,*[1] which takes place in the Wall Street district in the 19th century, Herbert Melville depicts the extraordinary destiny of an ordinary clerk. As a law-copyist Bartleby had to copy papers for the lawyer who employed him. A man of "pallidly neat, pitiably respectable, incurably forlorn" (p. 117) appearance he does his work, but one day he suddenly refuses to do his duty, simply declaring: "I would prefer not to." Nothing more than this dry sentence, repeated in a stereotypical way, bare of any reason which could open a dispute. The story takes its irresistible course. The clerk's refusal to serve continues with a refusal to eat when he is brought to a house for vagrants. The story ends where it began. We are told that earlier he had worked in a Dead Letter Office where letters that could not be delivered to their addressees were annually burnt. "Dead letters! Does it not sound like dead men? Conceive a man by nature and misfortune prone to pallid hopelessness: can any business seem more fitted to heighten it than that of continually handling these dead letters, and assorting them for the flames? [...] On errands of life, these letters speed to death" (p. 155). This story defies any kind of understanding and agreement we might take for granted. It takes place on the margins of dialogue, close to muteness, close to death. Such a refusal of response reminds us that dialogue also has its genealogy which for its part is not consensual.

* * *

Intentionality, Regularity, and Responsivity

A phenomenon like the alien, which shows itself only in eluding us, could be characterised as a kind of *hyperphenomenon*. Something which appears as this or that — as a chair or a locomotive, as a moon or a cherry blossom, as a boy or a girl, as an act of respect or an act of violence — is always more than and other than what it seems to be, since it is endowed with horizons of sense and symbolically overdetermined. It is precisely the "itself" of showing itself, the *Sich* of the *Sichzeigen*, that does not appear in what shows itself. Painting that tries to make visible the event of something showing itself turns into the "indirect painting" evoked by Merleau-Ponty in his essay *Eye and Mind* (1964a, p. 75). Such a painting makes visible what is invisible without depriving it of its invisibility. We are again reminded of a Japanese author. In his *Praise of the Shadows* Junichiro Tanizaki describes how the indirect illumination, so popular in Japanese everyday culture, grants things the distance they need in order to appear. So we may wonder what phenomenology looks like when it tries to show what does not appear itself. How should phenomenology proceed when confronted with an incarnate absence, a *leibhaftige Abwesenheit*?

It seems to me beyond doubt that intentionality, which was introduced into contemporary philosophy by Brentano, is one of the main features of phenomenology, and even animates hermeneutic and analytic philosophy, is not enough. By itself, it does not leave sufficient room for the alien as the alien. Intentionality means that *something* is intended or understood *as something*, that it is taken in a certain sense. Anything that might be alien would be previously conceived in such a way that it is reduced to some *part of a sense-whole*, even if it may be true that it manifests itself only bit by bit and never completely. Understanding turns out to be a special kind of appropriation, trying to overcome alienness by understanding, as Hans-Georg Gadamer explicitly claims in his great work *Truth and Method* (1965, p. 365). Understanding appears as a peculiarly sublime way of appropriation; it is supposed to be able to make everything appear as itself by overcoming its alienness or otherness, by making it familiar i.e. by receiving it, so to speak, into the bosom of one's own family. By contrast, anyone who insists that there is something alien which evades understanding seems to fall into the trap of a performative self-contradiction, trying to make understandable what is frankly stated to be beyond understanding. However this rather meagre argument betrays itself; it betrays exactly how the absence of what is alien turns into the negativity of something that is without sense as long as the alien is incorporated into the reign of sense.

Alienness does not fare better when it gets caught in the machinery of regularity, served by the various theories of communication and corroborated by linguistic analysis. Measured against rules to which all speech and action comply, what the Other says appears as a *case of a rule system* which regulates the Other's speech as well as one's own. Whereas intentionality tends to integrate the alien into a community of sense, we now pass beyond the own and the alien.[2] The levelling of the difference between the own and the alien does not stop when — as usually happens — one grants an open and variable form of rule compliance. Even deviations from rules are not sufficient; as long as nothing more receives attention than the mere deviation from rules, they relate to a virtual compliance to rules. From this perspective the strange seems to be nothing more than that which will be familiar tomorrow.

Nevertheless, even if Husserl's treatment of the phenomenon of the alien remains highly ambiguous, his work opens certain paths beyond the pure sphere of sense based on one's own intentions or on common rules. In this context I am especially interested in Husserl's theory of affection.[3] This theory consists of heterogeneous elements that are derived from various traditions, the Aristotelian, the Kantian and even the Fichtean tradition, and these elements do not automatically harmonise with each other. (1) Within the static perspective of *Ideas I* (see §§ 85–86), affection (in the Kantian sense) remains restricted to the task of providing material from which objects are built or constituted. From a dynamic point of view the materials enter into the teleology of the conscious life and contribute to the process of sense formation. Whatever is given is given as something. Not unlike Aristotle's πρώτη ὕλη, pure *hyle* has to be understood as a function, not as a primary datum. (2) The form-giving, goal-orientated process in and by which something appears as something appears to itself in a special sort of self-appearance such that our consciousness of something is accompanied by a special kind of self-awareness. Otherwise the appearance of something as something would fall back to the status of something occurring in the world. There is no affection without self-affection. A stimulus which is "alien to me" (*ichfremd*)[4] presupposes a self to which it is alien. In being affected I co-affect myself. A certain self-referentiality is already to be found in Aristotle's *philautia*, inherent in every form of *philia*, or in Rousseau's *amour de soi*, a self-feeling of living beings which has to be distinguished from the self-centred form of *amour propre*. This self-referentiality returns and is deepened in various ways in phenomenological analyses, for example in Husserl's doctrine of the primary impression (*Urimpression*), which was radicalised by Levinas; in the analysis of temporal self-affection which Heidegger carries out in his book on Kant; or in the hylic phenomenology of Michel Henry, which revolves on a supposed immanence of life, living and the sensing of itself by itself.[5] (3) The reversal of the reference to oneself is the reference to the alien. What is alien *to me* (*ich*fremd) presents itself simultaneously as *alien* to me (ich*fremd*). On this third level one gets a glimpse of some quasi-dialogical, or to put it in better terms, responsive aspects. I prefer the second formulation. It seems to me more appropriate because the hiatus between affection by the alien and affection by myself is not previously bridged by mutual understanding, based on views and opinions that we share. Pain which overwhelms us has no meaning in itself, although it can be interpreted afterwards as a symptom of bodily disturbances or physical defects. Affection by what is alien to me becomes crucial in Husserl's reflections on intersubjectivity. Husserl mentions doing to (*An-tun*) i.e. an af-fection in its literal sense, or being approached by something other what matters to us (*An-gang*), and he repeatedly refers to an appeal (*An*-ruf).[6] What is at stake here as the "alien to me" is not a mute non-ego nor another ego; it is that from which I start when I experience something as something and myself as someone. Heidegger, who devoted increasing interest to the "call" of conscience and to the "call" of Being, circumscribes experience as "das Zustoßende (what happens to me), An-gehende, Af-fektion."[7]

These are traces of another phenomenology. They indicate a sort of responsivity which exceeds the sphere of intentional or rule-dependent sense.[8] It is this excess which stimulates the response to the Other's demand, a response which neither has meaning nor follows given rules; on the contrary, it interrupts the familiar formations of sense and rule, provoking new ones. That *with which* I respond owes its meaning to the challenge *to which* I respond. The alien which hides itself in the Other's demand loses its alienness if the *responsive difference* between that to which we respond and that which we answer is levelled in favour of an intentional or rule-guided meaning process. The responsive difference disappears behind a *significative* or *hermeneutic difference* in which something is apprehended or understood as something, and behind a *regulative difference* in which something is treated according to a norm.[9] Instead the alien as alien requires a responsive form of phenomenology that begins beyond meaning and rules. It begins at the point where something challenges us and puts our own possibilities into question, even before we get involved in a questioning, in striving for knowledge, and in a will to know. This radical way of responding, inherent in whatever we say or do, undermines the traditional priority of questioning. That does not mean that we replace the traditional priority with another one. Mere reversals never lead very far. What we need is a shifting of weight and a new orientation. In each speech event dwells a certain promise that escapes from the conformity of regular conduct. Hölderlin's "we are a conversation" (seit ein Gespräch wir sind), so often invoked by the advocates of dialogue and communication, arises from the remoteness of the alien whose demands precede all partnership.

Demand and Response

Demand and response are the two key concepts I make use of in developing a responsive kind of phenomenology. In the demand of the Other, which breaks the purposive circle of intentionality as well as the circle of regulation or of communication, the alien emerges *in actu.* This kind of demand or *Anspruch,* as I would put it in German, means two things at once: a claim or pretension *to something* and an appeal directed *to someone.* Peculiar to the demand of the Other is the fact that both forms of *Anspruch,* i.e. claim and appeal, are combined just as the German term suggests. In the appeal I receive there arise claims that demand something from me, as when somebody asks me: "What time is it?" or "What is your name?" Incorporated into the situation, such demands precede every moral or legal claim. The question of whether a demand is legitimate or not presupposes that it is has already been received as an appeal. To take one of Kant's favourite examples, somebody who wants to avoid the duty to give back something that was deposited with him could simply avoid accepting deposits. Without loaning and borrowing there would be nothing to return. Many moral or legal obligations are contingent on preconditions, which for their part are not strictly regulated. Someone who keeps silent can hardly become a liar. But what if somebody wants to extract words from you? Here we reach a point *on this side of good and evil, of right and wrong,* where morality displays something like a blind spot.[10] All attempts to found morality presuppose factual demands which are more than mere facts. The simple occurrence of someone asking me for directions or asking for my name only becomes a fact when it is treated as a fact. This may happen along the lines of observing how someone asks me, stating that someone asks me, or recounting that someone did so. But something which *becomes* a fact *is not* a fact. The attempt to reduce the Other's question to a matter of fact cannot prevent me from being touched by the question. Moreover, responding does not begin with talking about something, it does not begin with talking at all, but instead with a sort of looking-at and of listening-to which to some extent is inevitable. Thus, I cannot hear the imperative "Listen!" without listening to it. The order "Do not listen to me!" leads to the famous double-bind: however one reacts, one reacts in the wrong way. Even attempting not to listen (*Weghören*) presupposes a certain listening, and attempting not to look (*Wegsehen*) presupposes a certain looking, just as Nietzsche's disrespect (*Verachtung*) includes a certain respect or regard (*Achtung, Beachtung*).

If we now pass to the kind of responding which corresponds to the twofold demand, we notice that our responding likewise takes on a twofold form. The answer I give corresponds to the claim, so when asked "What time is it?" I answer "Five o'clock." In terms of speech-act theory this has to do with the appropriate *answer content* to fill in the blank in the propositional content of questions or requests. Such an answer remedies a lack. Within the scope of so-called interrogative logic, the question can be construed to be an open sentence such as "It is x o'clock" which is completed by the information the answer delivers. The possibility of answering depends on a certain set of knowledge. If the required knowledge is at hand the answer somebody is looking for can be given by an answering machine which is based on a set of information and the corresponding operational rules. The automation of the inquiry-office or the use of translation machines are simple examples of this. But the very *event of responding* is in no way confined to this. Corresponding to the appeal addressed to me there is a response that does not fill a gap, but comes to meet the offers and demands of the Other. Responding in the full sense does not give what it has, but rather what it finds and invents in responding. Responding is distinguished from the answer given in a way similar to how denial is distinguished from negative propositions. Refusing to respond occurs at the level of the enunciation (*énonciation*) or the saying, not on the level of the enunciated (*énoncé*) or the said. Giving an answer is not exhausted by the answer given. The given answer can be adopted by the answering machine mentioned above, which then appropriately reacts to a suitable inquiry. But this would not do service as the giving of an answer — or refusing to give one — except in the case of a prefabricated dialogue in which answers are simply triggered or called up like data.[11] A machine that stops working is, however, not refusing to offer its service, and a machine whose programme has been enriched by phrases such as "Thank you for asking me" would not be being polite, although sometimes we may be inclined to be grateful to a machine that functions perfectly.

The doubling of the response into the responding event and the responsive content is clearly illustrated by the fact that I can quite properly respond to a question with a counter-question i.e. with a response which is not an answer in the sense of furnishing the information that another person is asking for. As we say in German, *Keine Antwort ist auch eine Antwort,* or in English: no answer is also a response.

Finally, responding that meets the Other's demand coincides in no way with spoken utterances. In the fulfilment of a request there is often a direct transition from the Other's speech into one's own action, for example when I do what I am requested to do. Furthermore, one can provoke with a glance and reply to glances. Clashing gazes are part of everyday life in large cities. Responding embodies an ethos of the senses that extends from grand ceremonies down to play between lovers. In the end the old dictum: "The human being is an animal which possesses discourse or speech" can be reformulated as: "The human being is an animal which responds." In this sense the difference between human and animal, as well as that between human and machine, must be reconsidered.

What looks like a generalisation of verbal forms of responding after the fact constitutes in reality a pervasive and prior feature of all our behaviour. Responses prove to be no less elementary than intentions and rules. As far as the context of discovery is concerned, the responsive phenomenology that I have tried to develop was inspired by the concept of *response* used by continental behaviour theorists such as K. Bühler, J. F. F. Buytendijk, W. Köhler and K. Lewin, who were still completely free of the shortcomings of Watson's or Skinner's behaviourism. Just as the demand is more than a mere causal stimulus, the response is more than a mere causal effect. As for the term *responsivity*, it can already be found in 19th century German medicine where it is used to describe the reciprocal exchange between the organism and its environment. Kurt Goldstein, a German-Jewish neurologist whose major work *Der Aufbau des Organismus* could only be published in the Netherlands in 1934 owing to the author's forced emigration, and was later translated into French and English, defines illness as "defective responsiveness" of an organism which is unable to meet the requirements of vital situations in an adequate way.[12] Later I discovered something similar in the writings of Mikhail Bakhtin. He also complements the traditional concept of *responsibility* with a more basic form of *answerability* (in Russian: *otvetnost'*) by which we do not render account for what we have said or done, but through which we take up what comes from Others (Bachtin 1979, p. 233). Philosophers would do well to search for nourishment not only inside but also outside their established discipline, since philosophy is also a type of responding.

Singularity and Inevitability

Responsivity, taken as a main feature of human behaviour, calls for a special logic of response that differs considerably from the logic of intentional acts, from the logic of understanding, or from the logic of communicative action. It leads to a specific form of rationality, namely a rationality which arises from responsivity itself, just as the logic of research arises from research itself. Therefore I shall conclude this lecture by pointing out some aspects of this peculiar logic, and by showing in each case how traditional themes begin to shimmer in the light of responding.

First, the demand of the Other is more than a part of a whole and more than a case of law: it takes on a specific form of *singularity*. This singularity indeed appears in the plural,[13] but in such a way that it eludes the distinction between the particular and the universal. Such a singularity does not mean that something occurs only once, such as for instance a sound or a crime. Nor does singularity mean that something is classified as one single case among others. We are not dealing with the individual which, according to the traditional view, is *ineffable* because it appears on the lower margin of an all-encompassing universality. Rather, we have to deal with a singularity of events which appear as such in that they deviate from familiar events and inaugurate a different seeing, thinking, and acting. In the life of individual persons as well as in the life of whole peoples and cultures there are key events (*Schlüsselereignisse*) or foundations (*Stiftungen*) "which one does not forget" (as Kant said with regard to the French revolution).[14] They are not forgotten because they introduce symbolic orders, establish meanings, and create new obligations i.e. they belong to what we are and have to be. In this regard the French revolution was, at least for participating Europeans like Kant, not one revolution among others; this uniqueness made it the crystallising point for various myths and rites. It is only when it is regarded through the eyes of a third party that the French revolution appears alongside the American, the Russian or the Chinese revolutions as one among others, just as a child, once it has grown, learns to regard its mother as a woman among other women and its birth place as a place among other places.

Likewise, the Other's demand does not fall within the disjunction between facts and norms, between is and ought, which since Hume and Kant has dominated the field of practical philosophy. The demand that makes itself seen, heard, thought and felt appears with a sort of *inevitability*, a *ne-cessitudo* in the literal sense, as something which cannot be derived from universal laws but which — as a practical necessity — belongs to the essential presuppositions of our common existence in the world. This inevitability means that I cannot not respond to the Other's demand once I am touched by it —just as, according to Paul Watzlawick's theory of communication (see Watzlawick and others 1967), I cannot not communicate. Not-responding would also be a sort of responding. The double negation that lies in the fact that I cannot not respond is known from modal logic's determination of necessity.[15] It refers to requirements which are grasped only indirectly, namely as insurmountable presuppositions which are implied in given experiences without being derived in a positive way. Along similar lines Kant posits a "fact of pure reason" (*Critique of Practical Reason*, A 56), Husserl a "necessity of fact" (Hua III, 109) or later an "absolute fact" (see below p. 101), and Sartre a "necessity *de facto*" (1943, p. 307). Due to its radicality, the demand of the Other evokes similar examples drawn from great traditions, such as the striving for happiness, the drive of self-preservation, the categorical imperative and human freedom. In Plato's view it is not up to ourselves to strive for happiness, just as for Kant it is not up to our discretion whether we hear the voice of the moral law or not. That from which our discourse and speech begins and has always already begun cannot be observed, judged, or managed as something lying before our eyes or in our hands. It only comes to light *while* we say and do something. It is dependent upon an indirect manner of speaking and communicating which remains connected to silence. This also holds true for the attraction that radiates from the alien and especially from an alien culture. Certainly there are learning processes that take place between cultures as soon as the stage of an "intercultural dialogue" is reached. However, one has as little control over such an attraction as one has over wonder or madness or love. As far as such upheavals are concerned, one can only yield to them or withdraw from them.

Posteriority, Asymmetry, and the Third Party

The two following aspects have to do with the specific form of temporality which connects and disconnects demand and response, and with a certain unevenness which prevents the two from being unified and integrated. The *diachronicity* of events undermines the *synchronicity* of sense by which the traditional *dialogue* is maintained. The dia- of the dialogue changes in the light of demand and response.

Singular events do not only raise inevitable demands, they also appear with an unreachable *previousness* (*Vorgängigkeit*). Correspondingly our response arrives with an original *posteriority* (*Nachträglichkeit*). This strange sort of delay cannot be understood by referring to successive positions on a time line. It does not only mean that something comes *earlier*, but that it comes *too early* to be anticipated here and now. It undermines the primacy of an originary presence. This presence is not nothing — as a good many postmodern total dissipaters believe — but it is not complete in itself. Responding takes place here and now, but it begins elsewhere. According to Derrida, the *Nachträglichkeit* of what we become aware of only *après coup*, after the fact, leads to the fact that the originary appears only "by a replacement," namely supported by supplements that draw an endless series of "originary repetitions" behind them.[16]

The same *Nachträglichkeit* leaves its mark on those traumatic accidents that can only be grasped in their after-effects, as Freud shows in the Wolfmann's childhood story. Speaking, as Habermas does (1973, p. 341), merely of a communicative distortion would be playing down the importance of what is at stake here. It would overlook the fact that the establishment of a communicative field no more takes place by communicative arrangement than is the constitution of a country itself introduced in conformity with the constitution and compliance integrated into the articles of the constitution. The foundation of an order is an event that does not function as a part of the order that it makes possible. In this respect each birth, which opens a new world, has something of a rebirth in it since it is only apprehensible in retrospect. Thus freedom means the ability not to begin absolutely with oneself but elsewhere. Whoever believes he or she is able to begin with him- or herself only repeats what already exists; in this way one does not begin. Responding means to renounce a first, and consequently also a last, word.

Going hand in hand with the temporal deferment of demand and response is an unavoidable *asymmetry* that throws traditional dialogue, which is orientated on common goals and follows common rules, out of balance. This asymmetry also leaves behind moral demands for equality such as the Golden Rule. As Levinas shows, this asymmetry does not depend upon the fact that in the course of an ongoing dialogue roles are distributed unequally; rather, the asymmetry depends upon the fact that demand and response do not converge. Between question and answer there is no more consensus than between request and fulfilment. The two collide like two glances that meet. Meeting the claim of the Other's demand and giving the gift of an answer only correspond to mutual giving and taking when one's own contribution and that of the Other are considered in the light of a *Third Party*.

But how does the Third Party intervene in our responding to the Other? This additional question is a highly important one. It touches on the link between the *Otherness* of the Other, which creates a certain distance between me and him or her, and the *sociality* of all of us, which encompasses whatever we have in common. Referring alternatively to the figures of the Other and the Third Party, I do not want to suggest that the two figures are similar to two sides of a coin or to two aspects of the same thing, capable of being integrated into a whole. On the contrary, they in no way fit into one and the same configuration because they point in different directions and open different dimensions.

Let us begin with the figure of the Third Party. From Simmel to Sartre,[17] the Third Party is well known as a *third person* who observes the dialogical sequence going on between me and thee, or who intervenes in social interaction as an arbiter, leader or co-ordinator. However the third person does not only speak for him- or herself. He always speaks in the name of common rituals, linguistic rules or public laws. This *anonymous Third Party* is entangled with the personal one, as in the case of the father, speaking, as Lacan puts it, "in the name of the father"[18] and playing the role of a super-ego. Now the most important point is the fact that the Third Party incorporates a more or less *general point of view* which comes from everywhere and nowhere. Notwithstanding factual restrictions, everybody can play the role of the Third Party and nobody can appropriate it. To put it in Husserlian terms: the Third Party is everybody (*jedermann*) as anybody (*jemand*) or anybody as everybody. To the extent that we claim the role of the Third Party, intersubjectivity shrinks to transsubjectivity, and interculturality shrinks to transculturality because it does not matter who speaks or acts in a general way. We take the Third Party's point of view whenever we try to understand *the other person* or another culture, referring to general sense-structures or sense-rules, and all the more do we adopt the Third Party's position when trying to come to terms *with others* in case of dissent or conflict. Consequently, human rights are considered as everybody's rights. What the universal claims to validity (*Geltungsansprüche*) that Habermas refers to, and the universal structures of the life-world that Husserl takes recourse to, have in common is that they both transport us into a sphere beyond the own and the alien i.e. into a sphere of neutrality and indifference. Whereas the structures of Husserl's life-world are on this side of the difference between me and others, Habermas' claims to validity are on the other side.

Now I am far from rejecting general or even universal points of view, without which no order would be possible. But I strongly contest a certain trend of universalisation, and I do so in the name of the otherness of the Other and also of myself. To put it in very clear terms: *The point of view of universality* should not be confused with a supposed *universal point of view.* Even if members of a certain group, people or culture lay claim to the universal rights of man, they do so under certain conditions and with certain consequences. Contrary to what some political, religious or moral ventriloquists pretend, mankind has no voice of its own and nor do peoples. At best, someone is speaking in the name of such collectives.

But what about the other figure, the figure of the Other? This figure is eclipsed when we try to usurp a universal view of the world. From this universal point of view, the Other is reduced to a *particularised Third Party*, while the Third Party is elevated to the status of a *generalised Other.* Against this kind of confusion, we should keep in mind that the Other to whom we respond, when speaking, acting or behaving, is in a certain way *incomparable.* That does not mean that the Other approximates the value zero on a scale of comparison. If we were to argue in this way we would still be comparing the Other with others. On the contrary, the other person or even the other culture that attracts, repels, stimulates, provokes us, which contests the very life we live, including the possibilities of life we reject, this Other is beyond comparison. Responding *to the Other* differs radically from understanding *the Other* and coming to terms *with the Other.*

Considered as a whole, the viewpoint of the Third Party is indispensable. Insofar as in discourse and action certain forms are repeated and certain rules or laws are applied, there is always some third person or instance that transgresses individual standpoints and perspectives. However, by subjecting the Other's demand to a universal law and by thus *equalising what is not equal,* justice always contains a grain of injustice. In terms of Nietzsche there is no *Auslegung* (i.e. interpretation) without *Zurechtlegung* (i.e. arrangement, cf. "construction"). The attempt to produce a definitive symmetry between the own and the alien and to make both equal to each other would ultimately be similar to the attempt to balance present and past, waking and sleeping, or life and death —

as if one could cross the threshold that separates one from the other in either direction just as one liked. The alien does not allow this; it behaves like ideas that occur to us, like obsessions that haunt us, like dreams from which we never fully awaken. It originates from an irrevocable once upon a time and from an irrevocable elsewhere.

Responding to What Happens

Some concluding words about the creativity and the normality of our responding. Obviously there are answers at hand, embedded in the normality of customs and morals. But whenever and wherever the order of things and words is shaken, a gap opens between the provocation with which the Other confronts us and our response. Here we run into the paradox of a *creative response* which resembles Merleau-Ponty's paradox of creative expression.[19] The response is creative as a response i.e. as a form of saying and doing which begins elsewhere, without being grounded in a given sense or in existing rules. Creative responses are responses that are not pre-given, neither in the realm of things nor in the realm of words. Thus responding runs over a small ridge which separates bondage (*Hörigkeit*) from arbitrariness (*Beliebigkeit*). This means: whenever we respond, we invent to some extent that *which* we respond, but we do not invent that *to which* we are responding.

Responding constitutes our own speaking and doing, but it is a speaking and doing which arrives from elsewhere. As already suggested, Kant's famous definition of freedom as the "capacity to begin a state by oneself" (see *Critique of Pure Reason,* B 561) has to be re-formulated: "One begins, but coming from elsewhere." Whatever happens in this way goes beyond any capacity which would precede what has to be done. Being responsive in itself, freedom includes the fact that what becomes real always exceeds what was possible in advance. But that is not all. It is not enough to concede that *my saying and doing comes from elsewhere,* we have to admit further that *something/somebody comes to me.* Or to put it in other words: something occurs or happens to me in terms of pathos. I am indeed involved, but not as an author or an actor *who* fulfils an act, but as a patient *to whom* what happens happens. In this respect the human being is not only an "animal which has a *logos,*" but also an "animal which endures a specific *pathos.*"

Before explicitly taking up this issue let us take another look at Bartleby. The destiny of this marginalized figure does not only illustrate how human freedom passes from the pathos we undergo to the response we give. In addition to this, we discover a certain gap which opens between the one and the other. This gap can take the more intensive form of a cleaving or a blockade, as in the case of a trauma which leads to a fixation on what has happened, or in the case of a muteness which prevents us from responding to what happens. As long as the general state of the patient is cut off from the state of the respondent, one becomes a patient in the restricted clinical sense. This possibility belongs to the pathology of freedom, it has nothing to do with any relapse to the state of a mere animal. Our story of the Wall Street clerk clearly shows that becoming silent does not mean escaping completely from language. Someone who declares, "I would prefer not to" refuses to respond, but he does so nonetheless by responding, though in a minimal way. The door remains slightly ajar.

Lecture III

The Power of Events

Opening: *A traffic accident.* — Robert Musil's novel *The Man without Qualities*[1] starts with a description of an ordinary traffic accident, but what he presents is more than an ordinary description. In the beginning something occupies the scene, namely an abruptly braking lorry which has "jumped out of line" (*aus der Reihe gesprungen*), making a "sidewards movement" (*quer schlagende Bewegung*). Beside it is the driver, "grey like wrapping paper," trying to explain what had happened. The gazes of the approaching people sink into the "depth of the hole" where the victim is lying as if dead. Everybody is waiting for the ambulance — for this "competent help" which will treat this emergency as a regular case. In the meantime, an over-smart passer-by who has witnessed the event explains to the lady accompanying him what "too long a braking distance" looks like. The lady accepts these explications gratefully; "it was sufficient for her to see that this brought some order into the horrible incident and transformed it into a technical problem which no longer touched her immediately." For such things we have "social institutions" which do their job with admirable accuracy. "It was almost possible to come away with the correct impression that what had happened was a regular and orderly event." Indeed, everything was statistically acceptable. The passer-by remarks to the lady with him that in America there are 190,000 persons killed and 450,000 persons injured by cars every year. Thus in opening the novel the author presents, in a paradigmatic way, something which turns out to be not so much an event but the normalisation of an event. From the woman's perspective, passing by with her gentleman, nothing seems to remain but the "unjustified feeling of having experienced something special." Does this mean that events stir up much ado about nothing?

* * *

It is strange to note that there are terms which we generally do not miss as long as they do not exist but which develop a special attraction as soon as they do appear. The term "event" (*Ereignis, événement*) is one of these. Its origin seems to be quite inconspicuous, and it is used in various ways. As far as I know, nothing like "eventism" has yet come on the scene. Nevertheless, a watershed separates those kinds of thinking in which everything that pertains to the event plays a central role, and others in which all of this is almost completely lacking, apart from special considerations, pertaining to the theory of history or to formal ontology. This may depend on how experience is conceived and how much importance is attached to it. It is not my intention to make a contribution to the history of ideas, but it should be stressed that on the threshold between the 19th and the 20th centuries there were certain affinities between Husserl, Bergson and James[2] which they all understood as a search for a non-empiricist philosophy of experience. Such a philosophy implies a strong concept of experience i.e. a sort of experience which does not supply us with pure data but which organises, structures and forms itself without being governed by fixed laws. This explains its strong connection to the inventiveness of life which, due to the recent victory of the bio-sciences and bio-technologies, appears in a new light. What is at stake here is not only the attempt to avoid the stumbling blocks of rationalism and empiricism, taking and giving on both sides, but to question the assumption of *a priori* laws and *a posteriori* facts, looking for a happening which makes its own way and literally *er-fährt* something. The power of events we are referring to depends on the basic fact that their effects are earlier and stronger than any attempt to interpret, to explain or to change them.

We may ask why such a radicalisation of experience, giving rise to thought in terms of events, has had a much broader and deeper resonance in post-war France than in the English- and German-speaking countries. This seems to be all the more astonishing when we consider that the French thinkers concerned took and take different paths. Yet almost none of them has remained completely untouched by Husserl's phenomenology and Heidegger's thinking of Being. In my own contribution I will restrict myself to describing those constellations which prompted me to start using a new concept of event. It goes without saying that in my own efforts I frequent the German-French borderlands.

In what follows I first want to show the frictional surfaces which allow us to ignite sparks on the concept of event. In doing so I shall inscribe this concept into a tetragram corresponding to the four central problems of order, self, others and time-space. Tackling the problem in this indirect way makes it easier to avoid the less satisfying alternative of minor events, which are rather trivial, and great events, which are too sublime.[3]

Getting out of Line

Let us start in the field of order and history. In general, we call events historic if it is not only the case that something happens, but that what happens is something special and important. This qualification is one of the main topics of historiography and should not be taken for granted. In his famous novel Robert Musil, an author whom we could regard as a late modern sceptic of history, does not only suggest a man without qualities and qualities without man, he does not only speak of "experiences without somebody who lives them" (p. 150), he also refers to events without qualities which strictly speaking happen to nobody, as in case of the traffic accident with which we started. Something had happened that happens every day in a similar way. The headline of one of the sub-chapters is "Seinesgleichen geschieht": things of a kind happen. In a later passage, Ulrich, the protagonist of the novel, confronted with the events in the Balkans at the end of 1913 and the beginning of 1914, wonders whether what happened was really history. "Indeed, some intervention did take place, but he did not know whether it was really war that happened" (p. 359). His doubt refers to the comparability of events because taking place implies "that it happens itself and not something that is ultimately only something of the kind" (p. 360). But what does it mean to say that something takes place "itself"? Obviously it means that what happens is *more than a mere case of a rule*, which could be replaced by many other cases like it (*seinesgleichen*). It means that a question mark is placed after the general rule even if this rule is confirmed by what happens. The rule could be in force without any restriction only on condition that the given event is *nothing more* than a mere case i.e. if the dissimilar which *is* not the same, but only *becomes* the same, were to disappear behind the equalising effect of order.

These considerations are apt to produce a first wave of revision. From a modern, norm-orientated view one distinguishes between *order* (rules, structures or conditions of possibility), their *being in force*, and *facts* (states of affairs, processes or relations) *subject to order*. If this gulf between order and what is ordered is bridged by dialectics, this sort of mediation is achieved by reason and on the part of reason; the traditional coming to the essence, the γένεσις εἰς οὐσίαν (*Philebus* 26 d), turns out to be the coming of reason to itself. What is real is or becomes rational, or at least it obeys reason. The concept of event remains weak because one presupposes in advance the directives of a regulative or the totality of a substantial reason. An alternative arises if order itself is submitted to contingent conditions and if order itself happens. If we follow Leibniz, who assumes that the real miracle is the *miracle de raison*, something changes. There is not only something implicit which becomes explicit i.e. something folded which unfolds. On the contrary, the process of order drapes itself in folds so to speak. Consequently, what Husserl and Heidegger call foundation (*Stiftung*) has to be understood as an inaugural event which discloses new fields of sense by closing others, an event which makes things possible by making other things impossible. We have to admit that "there is" truth, sense, rationality and order, as Heidegger, Merleau-Ponty and Foucault put it. This sort of genealogy affects every kind of order, the order of logic as well as that of morals, politics and art.

Now a series of questions arise. First we have to question the uniformity of event. Do we not have to accept two kinds of event i.e. intra-ordinary events, which take place on the ground of a given order, and extra-ordinary events, which leave this ground behind and change it? Or in other words, do we not have to presuppose that there are conformable and normal events on the one hand, and deviating and anomalous events on the other hand? It seems to me that this kind of two-level happening, separating workday and everyday events from holiday events, simply reproduces the traditional split between ideality and reality, between legitimacy and facticity, and this has dubious consequences. As long as we admit such differences in such a way that they do not originate from the very process of order, events in the radical sense of the word do not exist. The alternative we have in mind looks rather different. There are not two classes of event, the one constituting as it were an upper class, the other an under class. Rather, what we find are different sorts of *dominance* and *polarisation*. An event may primarily contribute to the testing, to the consolidation or to the reproduction of a certain order, or it may directly participate in breaking or undermining the given order and replacing it with another. Whether the murder of the Austrian successor to the throne by a Serb nationalist, to which Musil alludes, will be more than a common, daily recurring accident or crime cannot be decided in advance. Every event is to some extent Janus-faced because it makes us look forwards and backwards. It does not depend much on the "leave" from public life that Ulrich has taken (p. 47) and on the observer's attitude he adopts when he tends to dampen great historical expectations affirming: "There were so many things moving mankind," and when he enumerates high-flight records, boxing championships, presidential journeys, the success of a tenor and earthquakes as if he were looking into a kaleidoscope (p. 359). But can we really say that these things move "mankind"? At this point another question arises. To whom do things of a kind happen? Before trying to answer this question we must concede the possibility that we are approaching a state which can be described as a deadlock or as rotation on the spot. Whenever nothing can be found which gives weight and colour to what happens, indeed nothing happens. The fading of differences leads to a dead-end in which the monotone grey of everyday approaches nothingness. Everyday becomes abysmal when reduced to pure everydayness. Beckett's dramas derive their force from the fact *that* nothing happens. They evoke a sort of waiting without any expectation: "Here I was sitting, waiting / waiting — but for nothing ..." (Nietzsche, *Sils Maria*). Should something happen nonetheless, it comes unexpectedly.

There is a further question concerning the manner of change. We have learned to mistrust the great *Haupt- und Staatsaktionen*, the Pomp and Circumstance that Marx mocked, and also to mistrust the Walhalla of great men of action. Nevertheless we have to consider a *double rhythm*. On the one hand we meet erosive, gradual displacements, changing the texture and the chain of events. This kind of change, situated on the scale of *longue durée*, includes not only economic processes but also linguistic transformations which are very rarely ordered by a fixed date. On the other hand, there are irruptive and eruptive forms of change. We would have to be deeply absorbed in reading the *Annales* to be able to regard events such as the earthquake of Lisbon, the outbreak of World War I, Black Friday when the Stock Exchange crashed, the so-called *Reichskristallnacht*, the Hungarian insurrection, the fall of the Berlin wall or the attack on the World Trade Centre as events belonging to a series. In terms of geology we have to distinguish between neptunian and vulcanian events;[4] in terms of literature we could speak of epic and of dramatic plots. In order to avoid again a simple dichotomy I propose to speak of *key events*. Due to their polymorphic depth, these events display a special force of disclosure; they literally lose track of their role. When such events take place the course of things does not merely shift from one side to the other, as when one simply changes one's position or one's partner, rather it deviates from itself. In the same way as intentionality and observance of rules are not acts, but only modes of acts, deviation is not a special event, but a mode of event.

Finally, we have to ask how is it possible to talk about something new without assimilating what is becoming with what exists. The answer to this question can be found in the event itself. It consists in a peculiar sort of *doubling*, exceeding mere bipolarity and also mere change of rhythm. The effect of this process of doubling is that the emerging order becomes registered in the existing order. The extraordinary which characterises the foundation of order returns to precisely the order it inaugurates. System theorists call this re-entry. So in the end all incisive events become located and dated, and we note: Lisbon 1775, Paris 1789, Sarajevo 1914, Budapest 1956, Berlin 1989, New York 2001 or Baghdad 2003. The topical and chronological data we register are more or less spread out. The outbreak of war or the slump of the Exchange cannot be located and dated as precisely as an assassination or an attack because growing complexity allows only for junction knots rather than centres. In this regard the tableau presented in Tolstoi's *War and Peace* differs from the intrigue knotted in *Anna Karenina*. The latter novel culminates in a train accident which is already foreshadowed in the first chapter. But whereas the first victim, a simple line-man, who leaves behind a large family, remains as anonymous as the victim in Musil's novel, the second victim has a name, well known to the reader when the disaster appears. It is the name of the title heroine who becomes the title victim. This brings us into a new circle of problems.

To Whom Something Happens

The question "What happens?" leads to the further question "To whom does what happens happen?" Some may object that this second question is not strictly necessary. The description of the "beautiful day in August 1913," preceding the presentation of the above-mentioned accident like an anonymous stage direction, seems to demonstrate that we are not forced to personalise what happened. The traffic accident stands out against a neutral background which is described in terms of a cosmo-technology: "Above the Atlantic there was a barometric minimum: it was wandering eastwards toward a maximum, lying over Russia." We would be making things too easy for ourselves if we were to point out that "Russia" is more than a meteorological co-ordinate and that the name of this huge country, linked up with the famous year, looks like a historical portent. There is always the possibility of expressing this in terms of degrees of longitude and latitude, banishing the very human joy about the beautiful weather to the private economy of feelings. However, even in this case there remains the meteorologist who is responsible for the weather service. As long as he does not embrace the barometer like a totem he may well be quite disinterested in what happens under the sun of this day in August, but this does not mean that he has no personal interests. Rather, he postpones them in the course of his professional duty. The pair of passers-by whom we have already met go somewhat further. The gentleman and his lady simply pass by, they observe what is going on and give their comments, but they are unable to deny a certain concern: "I hope he is still alive," the man replies to the woman who has her doubts about "having experienced something special." "When they lifted him into the car," he continues, "it looked like it." The ironic point of this concluding remark of the scene lies in the fact that the survival of the victim eliminates the residue of the "peculiar" pertaining to death, in spite of the levelling effect of all the numbers quoted. As far as the special feature of event is concerned, there is not much left. We may continue the normalising talk by coolly stating that ultimately even the question of life and death amounts to the question as to whose insurance has to pay. This way we would get back to where we have already been: on the ground of a given order. Certainly, we should not play off an emphatic form of one's own life and death against life and burial insurance or against any other kinds of accounting with life, as if accounts were nothing more than a nightmare. Such attempts at re-appropriation, elevating the proper in the sense of the own (*das Eigene*) to the proper in the sense of the authentic (*das Eigentliche*), always have a forced character, deriving their force from what they attack. Instead we have to face the question of whether orders in which things of a kind happen really become visible and sensible without being repeatedly shaken by what is nothing of the kind, and further, whether such a shaking of order is possible without somebody to whom something happens, who is involved in what happens. The feared death by accident would put this to a test. What is at stake here is not the pure narcissism of the old subject, which cannot get away from himself, but rather the fact that death as well as pleasure, pain and other affects move straight into the world of fiction if they lack somebody who experiences them. In this regard they resemble the grin of the Cheshire cat in *Alice in Wonderland.*

We do not have to ask whether somebody is involved in the events, but only how this is the case. Thus we get into a second wave of revision. Under the auspices of the modern subject another dichotomy arises which defuses the event in a new way. We have grown accustomed to positing on the one hand *objective, impersonal occurrences,* described from the observer's perspective, and on the other hand *subjective acts,* ascribed to somebody, or *personal actions,* for which somebody is responsible. It is no accident that the title of Donald Davidson's famous book is *Essays on Actions and Events. Actions* and *acts* are presented *as events* which become characterised by intentionality or regularity. As to feelings like anxiousness which are not intentionally directed towards something and do not violate rules, nothing remains other than the field of *mental states* which, having been scrupulously cleared of mines, are not so exciting. Actions of failure such as stumbling, stammering or simple sneezing as well as eruptions of laughing and weeping are labelled as physiologically conditioned reflexes or corporeal mechanisms which only accompany our expressive actions. Everything that does not find its place on the level of psychological or mental acts and states declines to the level of physical-corporeal *epiphenomena.* The provocative de-sublimation that Pascal achieves in ascribing a historically effective "malice of the object" to Cleopatra's nose is out of place here.[5]

The motif of event provokes a shift, similar to what we have found in the domain of rules and structures, inherent to given orders. It is important to ensure that the impersonal form of "it happens" is not hastily personalised. The fact that different authors emphasise the "it": "it thinks" (Lichtenberg, Nietzsche[6]), "it or one perceives" (Merleau-Ponty[7]), "it writes" (Calvino[8]), not to mention the "Es" instance in Freud which intervenes in all our thinking and volition without being restricted to a lower level of our soul, points to the very happening of experience. Throughout this happening something becomes visible, audible, sensible, in such a way that it comes to our mind, strikes us, attracts or repels us and withdraws from our knowing and willing, without being ascribed to a subject who would function as the author or bearer of acts and actions. Fields of experience organise themselves on their own, as gestalt theory has shown. Observation may be defined as an act, but not so the excitement of attention, which sets our experience in motion; pleasure and pain behaviour can be learned and governed, but not our feeling of pleasure and pain or our well-being or ill-being. Everything that happens to us, right up to the limit events of birth and death which are repeated in our life in different ways, may be called *pathos,* which is to be understood as what in German is called *Widerfahrnis.* We could also speak of an *af-fect* as long as the *An-tun, An-regen* or *An-rufen* is understood and as long as affects are not degraded to private states of feeling.

The formula "*it* happens" (es *ereignet sich*) can be read with another accent as "it happens *itself*" (*es ereignet* sich). Such an event refers to itself as indicated by reflexive verbs such as *sich freuen, sich bewegen* or *sich äußern.*[9] This *Sich* opens a fissure within the event. Without such a *Sich* the *Es geschieht* would be again reduced to an ordinary event we observe and manipulate from the outside — or it would be hypostasized and dynamised in terms of a purely self-referential *ipsum esse,* able to be evoked in a tautological way or to be used in a demagogic way: a happening happens, *il arrive.*

The interpretation of the event as pathos raises a series of further questions. First, we have to ask in what manner somebody who appeals to his own or to an outer pathos is involved. Our answer to this question, which may be able to put an end to the debate about the life or death of the so-called subject, is many-faceted. Using the grammatical form of the *dative*, we ascribe the fact that something happens to me or to you, to him or to her, to an instance which precedes the possibility of saying *I* or even of positing a *Me*; nevertheless, what happens does not shift to the third-person perspective. The disjunction between a first-person or a third-person perspective, to which even contemporary neurology appeals, should be taken as a useful methodical instrument albeit one of limited range. Expressions such as *es geschieht, it happens*, which belong to the linguistic category of the impersonals, should not be interpreted as the negation of the personal but as a diffuse ascription which does not presuppose a steering centre. In his *Theory of Language* (1982, p. 376, Engl. p. 428) Karl Bühler calls weather words like "raining," formed by defective rather than full-scale verbs, event words (*Ereigniswörter*); he presumes that they open up a different symbol world because in phrases like "It is raining" the questions "Where?" and "When?" are the leading questions, not the question "Who?". It could have a liberating effect for us Europeans if we were to take notice of extra-European languages where the sentence structure is not so strongly centred on the grammatical form of the subject and where the verb has much more play compared to the noun. Perhaps one should make a further step, asking whether our grammatical distinction between noun and verb, between ὄνομα and ῥῆμα (see Aristotle, *De interpretatione* 3) is not all too rigid. Single words, taken from more classical Chinese, such as "cows with black lips," "cows without horns," "cows mooing" or "cows breathing" do not only depict states of affairs, as Tze-wan Kwan puts it, they also depict movements or events, changing a being (the cow) into something moving (something like "cowing"), as if the noun became a verb. Of course this would be a transcription into Western categories, but it is more than just a transcription because these categories then start oscillating themselves.[10]

The dative structure of what happens to me or to you leads to the suspension of some other distinctions. Let us begin with the distinctions between the *own* and the *alien*, between *action* and *passion*. What happens to me is from the beginning interspersed with what is alien to me, with *Ich-Fremdem* as Husserl puts it. This alien reaches my very core, so that speaking of "my pain," of "my pleasure" or generally of "my body" seems to be only an unavoidable *façon de parler.* What happens to me is anything but my action, but on the other hand it is not a mere passion either, taken in the sense of a reversed action which I spontaneously impute to another agent or actor. But in order to do that I should have to change to the other side and to observe myself from the outside, something which can be achieved only in an indirect and highly mediated way. We may call what precedes all these possibilities primary passion (*Urpassion*), a sort of "being affected by ...," which escapes from the usual schemes of spontaneity and receptivity, of action and passion.[11] In his studies on passivity Husserl was on the track of that original form of passivity, and French authors such as Merleau-Ponty and Levinas have continued on this path. The pathos-orientated form of phenomenology which I am elaborating continues these attempts.

Finally, we have to ask how what happens to me affects me as somebody who bears a *name* or as somebody who remains *anonymous.* The "It" (*Es*) we are considering takes the form of a "One" (*Man*) which requires a syncretistic kind of imputation, a greater or lesser degree of co-operation i.e. a measured sort of responsibility, not to be confused with dispensation from responsibility. Events in which we are involved in special ways are inscribed into a social field i.e. into an intermediary domain which can be neither distributed to individuals nor integrated into a whole. The old opposition between individualism and holism, which only oscillates between actors on the small and on the large scale, fails as soon as what "happens to us and with us" originates from the individualising and generalising effect of this very happening. We cannot skip the question as to *who* has the experience, but this question receives its answer in the very process of experience. Individuals as well as collectives are constituted, they are not a fundamental given.

As to the relationship between event and *act* or *action,* every kind of simple dichotomy misses the point—just as in the case of ordinary and extra-ordinary events. What happens to us *becomes* an act or an action, but only to some extent i.e. as far as it is ascribed to somebody. The question remains to what extent this is possible. In the presentation of Moosbrugger, in which Musil's search for a man without qualities enters the legal field, this question plays a crucial role. Moosbrugger, a tramp charged with the murder of a prostitute, acknowledges the death sentence with the paradoxical affirmation: "I am satisfied with that, even if I have to concede that you have sentenced a madman." After having followed the trial breathlessly, Ulrich concludes: "This was clearly madness, and also a distorted union of our own elements of being." This all looks "piecemeal and completely obscure" to him "as if mankind as a whole were dreaming" (p. 76). The transformation of the *To Whom* of pathos to the *Who* of response, and simultaneously the transformation of an event into an act or an action, raises further questions. In the twilight of the clinic and the court, in the double refraction by pathology and criminology, they are only intimated. We are accustomed to dealing with them in terms of the constitution *of the self.* But the paradox which lurks in the double reading of the genitive refers to a sort of happening which Husserl cautiously conceives as *Sichkonstituieren.*

What Happens between Us

The trial, drawn upon as an example, implies that the *Widerfahrnis,* what happens to me, is not only multiple but that the *Widerfahrnisse* pass over into each other, producing sequences of events which cross each other. Even for this complication our tradition offers certain concepts. There is the *alter ego,* the Other or Others. Something like an inter-subjectivity arises as soon as several subjects join each other in terms of interactions and interlocutions, with the effect that my own words and actions are connected with those of the Others. But ultimately, we have to deal with a sort of inter-subjectivity and interaction without the "inter." The problem of the other and the alien has been already defused before being settled, and this is so because what happens between us is ascribed in advance to a subject or person, conceived as a source of experience, as an author or as an bearer of rights. In this regard it makes no great difference whether one derives this interplay from individuals, moved by their own interests, drives and visions or by repressed wishes and wish projections, or whether one assumes a co-ordinating centre through which the one refers to the other as if the one were to take the other's place.

However, the motif of event stirs up a new and third wave of revision by which the social distribution of sense and duality, clearly separating the own and the alien, is undermined. In the course of my own social philosophical attempts I first introduced an intermediary realm (*Zwischenreich*) and later on, in order to leave more place for dispersion, this common domain was multiplied into intermediary events (*Zwischenereignisse*). In this way I tried to understand how something happens between us which can neither be reached by summarising individual achievements, nor reduced to a unifying centre, but able to create and grant something we have in common. In this context I draw a distinction between what we generally call connection (*Verknüpfung*), presupposing a mediating instance, a certain syn- which is well known in terms such as synthesis or synopsis and which sustains the process of understanding each other and of coming to terms with each other, and an open form of linkage (*Anknüpfung*). This latter means that somebody to whom something happens responds to something other in such a way that what he or she answers does not have sufficient reasons in what is and what ought to be. Our response can turn out this way or that way, it can be refused or given, the refusal being itself a sort of responding. The "and-so-on" of a verbal or practical sequence, following such a response, can never be transferred into a definitive "therefore." Intermediary events which always come from elsewhere and always lead elsewhere prevent us from posing a first or a last event. There is an *entretien* in the fullest sense only if between what happens to me and how I respond there is a hiatus interrupting the flow of words and actions, even when I speak to myself.[12] It is not enough to assume that we encounter breaks in speech and action where the pendulum shifts; strictly speaking nothing happens unless a gap is traversed which separates af-fects from ef-fects. This gap leaves space for interventions which are more than the pure product of our own already existing wishes and visions.

The between which connects us with each other and simultaneously separates us from each other can be radically conceived only in terms of a *self-doubling in the Other* i.e. as a lived impossibility, im-possible measured on the possibilities which are available for me, for you and for us altogether. I *am* where you cannot be, and you *are* where I cannot be, as Paul Celan's verses persistently suggest. This distance-in-proximity and proximity-in-distance, which is put to a special test by the gender difference, touches the motive of the double. The abysses of doubling manifest themselves again in the figure of Moosbrugger. He feels persecuted by his female victim as by his own shadow, and suddenly he realises "that he will never get away from her because he was himself dragging her behind himself," that "soft, damned second ego" which lies down beside him and which he finally attacks with his knife (p. 74). Taking up Musil's formula we can state: "the likes of me (*meinesgleichen*) happens"; but here the uncanny (*das Unheimliche*) lurks which stirs me up in my very core, where I am at home. In this context, Paul Valéry also refers to the motive of the double when he writes in his *Cahiers* (vol. I, p. 499): "The Other, the like of me, or maybe my double, that is the most magnetic abyss." An attraction emanates from him, a force which does not transport a hidden sense and which escapes from our own doing, withdrawing our ground from us. The author continues: "Rather ape than imitator — reflex which responds, precedes, amazes." What is crucial is the precedence which is not only the mark of special surprising effects, but which distinguishes the event from any search and any rule-following.

What Takes Place and Proceeds

Our last step shall approach the riddle of time, which presents itself as a sort of time-space. Again, nothing is achieved by ascribing temporal and local qualities to events. On the contrary we have to conceive time from the vantage of the event before submitting it to temporal and spatial schemes. The decisive moment has already been mentioned. To say that something happens implies that it contrasts with itself, that it separates and splits itself from itself, that it flees from itself. The volatility of time does not primarily mean that something passes away, but that it escapes from itself, and the dispersion of the spatial does not primarily mean that something is dispersed through space, but that something places and locates itself. If we may assume that events can be brought to language, then this is only by virtue of a temporal-spatial diastasis, inherent to the event.

Once more we have to be on our guard against a common interpretation which misses the mark in two ways. First, one orientates oneself either on something which is *no longer*, but reconnects the event to its origin, or one orientates oneself on something which is *not yet*, but promises to bring the event to its goal. Consequently, what happens *here and now* is nothing more than the passage from the no-longer to the not-yet. But to assume that something happens, that it gets out of line, that it happens to me or to you or between us without being pre-seeded, can only mean that the event deviates from itself, displaces itself, folds itself, moves in a sinuous line. "Crooked line — victory of free nature over the rule," as Novalis puts it (*Schriften*, vol. II, p. 157). That means that the event is other than what it is, that it is somewhere else than where it is, that it happens to somebody who is somebody else than he or she is.

Compared to the expectations we have, everything that happens to us comes too early, just as every response we give comes too late. This original delay does not only affect the experience of the individual as emerging from the Other, it also affects the relationship between generations and eras. Pre- and post-history are intertwined, constituting a "history of syncopes in which the moments of burial and resurrection are pre-eminent."[13] This constitutive non-simultaneousness constitutes a kind of future which means more than prolonging, improving or worsening what already exists here and now. We return to what is coming in terms of the future perfect to which various authors refer. What we call the present nests in the fissure between previous pathos and posterior response. This fissure will never be closed, but from the beginning it is overshadowed by oblivion and it will never cease to sink into oblivion. This is not only the case where one clings to existing orders, but also where one turns the event into an "Event" to be sought for. What is impending, what is coming to meet us, will be found before it is looked for.

Lecture IV

Time-Lag

Opening: *No first word, no last word.* — Is there a first word? Jorge Semprun's novel *What a Beautiful Sunday*, the first chapter of which is entitled "Zero," begins as follows: "He had the feeling he had perceived a vague movement. Some sort of crunching of whirled up snow." Is this how the novel begins? Certain things have already happened before the narrative starts. *Quel beau dimanche*! Which Sunday? A Sunday in Buchenwald. Some sort of crunching? "Maybe beneath the wheels of a truck at the fork in the road in the barracks." And so it proceeds, forwards and backwards. A first word would be one that responds to nothing: not to an idea, not to terror, not to an allure ...

And a last word? At the end of the novel the narrator starts exchanging words with a fellow captive whom he calls "Jehovah." He breaks off this conversation because he fears an "appropriate Bible verse." "There must be many beautiful, appropriate Bible verses on darkness. But I didn't feel like having something about darkness read to me in Jehovah's voice. I just prefer Giraudoux.... I feel like spending the rest of this Sunday with him" — this Sunday, which will be followed by others. So no last word. The last word would be one that permitted of no further expectation, that had no harassment to fear, that no one could call into question...

* * *

The time-lag in question here may be understood in two ways: as a shift in time itself, and as a corresponding shift in signification. The following considerations begin with a general orientation as to the ordering of time; then they cross over to specific phenomenal fields in which time unfolds its effect. When speaking about the previousness of the pathos and the posteriority of the response we were permanently confronted with the effects of time. As we will now see, the dynamic of time includes a specific sort of othering.

Logos of Time

The logos of time is to be understood as the way we think of time, talk about it, represent it and present it, and all of this with reference to an experience of time that like all phenomena is to be brought "to the pure expression of its own meaning." (Hua I, 77)

The oldest discourse on time is found in *myth.* Chronos is known as a god who devours his own children, a god older than Zeus. Here time is portrayed as a power that in coming to be and passing away, in ageing, manifests itself as a deterioration and disintegration of forces. Some of this lives on in poetry: "Make haste Chronos! Out of the rattling trot!" — in Goethe Chronos is apostrophised as a coachman and entreated in his distant proximity. In Virginia Woolf's *Mrs. Dalloway* it is Big Ben's chime that scans the course of the day within the novel.[1] Or finally Octavio Paz in his poem *Piedra del Sol*: "*mientras el tiempo cierra su abanico* [while time folds its fan shut]" (1987, p. 11). Thus the influences and consequences of time prove to be much older than the logos, which responds to the work of time, seeking to reclaim an order from this work.

The *classical ordering of time* that has determined our thinking for centuries develops particular coping strategies that work against time's power. Three fundamental aspects of this may be distinguished. (1) In the first place there is the attempt at a certain demythologisation. Time appears no longer as a who or what presided over by a time-sovereign or an anonymous temporal power; rather time appears as a how, as mode, as schema. Time débuts *in something* or *in someone*; it is no longer under its own direction. On the one hand Aristotle composes the great prelude: he derives a physical time from cosmic kinesis. On the other hand there is Augustine, who develops a psychological time from the lived time of the soul. This psycho-physical duality continues up to the present day. Time is cordoned off as long as the question "What is X?" or "Who am I?" does not *eo ipso* carry a temporal or spatial accent. What emerges in time is not something that temporalizes itself. In modern terms, identity does not immediately mean *temporal identity*, in the sense that today it is customary to speak of *spatial identity*. Identity remains timeless in its very core. (2) The mode of time is repeatedly subjected to *binary schemata of order*, such as outer and inner, physis and psyche, material and form. (3) Time itself is conceived as a *member of an opposition*. The most pointed oppositions are those between time and space (following one another in succession versus standing out from one another in extension), between time and eternity (flowing vs. standing, temporal flux vs. *nunc stans*). In this way the force of time is tamed: one is at the mercy of time as a human being, but not as a thinking being.

The classical ordering of time gradually gives way to a *radical experience of time*, the consequence of which is that the logos turns into a "logos of the aesthetic world" (Hua XVII, 297). This leads to a transformation of the classical representation of time. (1) Time is henceforth more than an attribute of things or a way of experiencing the soul; it is also more than the form of intuition for a transcendental subject. Time is no longer reduced to a mere modality, since it has a decisive part in the formation, shaping, and realisation of something (object), of someone (subject), and of meaning (order). These three aspects, still distributed among three worlds by Karl Popper, have their specific temporal manners of being. Temporality turns out to be a *generator of identity*. (2) Time no longer falls under binary schemata; it proves to be a *differing* in the sense of a holding up, shift, or postponement. (3) Time frees itself from the opposition to timeless instances; it becomes entangled in itself in the form of *self-reference* that leads to a self-doubling and self-duplication. Thus Husserl remarks at the beginning of his time lectures (Hua X, 22) "that the perception of a temporal object has itself temporality, that perception of duration presupposes duration of perception"; and Merleau-Ponty speaks in his later writings of a temporal "vortex."[2] Here a phenomenology of time emerges with increasing and varying radicality in which time is intertwined with what it determines: as consciousness of time and time of consciousness in Husserl; as being and time as well as time and being in Heidegger; as flesh/body of time and time of the flesh/body in Merleau-Ponty; as time of the Other and alterity of time in Levinas and Derrida; as time of narrative and narrated time in Ricœur.

Equally worth mentioning are authors in the human sciences such as Ludwig Binswanger, Eugène Minkowski, Erwin Straus and Viktor von Weizsäcker in whose work the pathology of time takes on particular weight. In a broader sense the attempts of Bergson and Whitehead to think lived time together with a modern biology or cosmology belong within this sphere as well. Finally we should point to the fact that the conception of time in classical physics, which in many ways also has a part to play in the philosophical theories of time, has itself undergone substantial revisions. For instance, the theory of relativity has done away with the representation of a temporal receptacle and an absolute time, and deals with time-spaces, with a dependence upon movement in the measuring of time. We come upon new forms of time, "upon times dependent on the internal state of a system, upon a time that is an operator" that lends the "arrow of time" a new significance (Prigogine/Stengers 1986, p. 246).

In what follows I shall restrict myself to looking for a way through the field of time experience, orienting the search according to two central problems tightly intertwined with one another. The one problem concerns the self-referentiality already mentioned, which is not only restricted to time but returns equally in phenomena such as body, language or self, and prevents a hierarchic ordering of the phenomena. The other problem concerns the indirect mode of access, required when something withdraws from precisely those orderings in which it is conceptually grasped. Here Wittgenstein's distinction should be remembered, the difference between saying and showing, which do not coincide; and the late Merleau-Ponty, who states with regard to philosophy that "*elle fait voir par des mots*" — that philosophy shows by words what does not permit of being directly said (Merleau-Ponty 1964b, p. 276 f., Engl. p. 266). It is hard to better formulate the task of a phenomenologist. In the same context Merleau-Ponty places philosophy alongside literature (as well as politics): this is the meaning of "no absolutely pure philosophical word." Philosophy works in parallel to the arts, which perform (*auf*führen) in colours, sounds, movements and scenes what philosophy demonstrates (*auf*weist). This does not signify a simple conflation of categories, but rather a considerable proximity that also finds expression in the phenomenological analyses of time. It comes across in the following spheres of problems, which one could ascribe to a kind of "minimal art of time."

Time of Speech

Since philosophy is concerned with making time visible in words, speech may stand at the beginning. The following considerations do not follow the route of a "linguistic turn," which discovers much but also conceals things of importance. They are not so much about a return to language as a penetration into language. As far as the time of speech is concerned, it takes place at different levels.

At the first level we are dealing with *time as spoken about*, which belongs to *what is said*. The tested means of a grammar of time belong to linguistic articulation. This begins with the tenses of the verb, of the ῥῆμα, which according to Aristotle "co-indicates" time.[3] It continues with the adverbs of time, such as now, just (now); today, this year; earlier, later; often, seldom etc., that have since been formalised in a temporal logic. If factors of time only belonged to the topic of speech, then speech itself — together with all its law-givers and authors — would remain intact. The logic of time has developed a variety of strategies for detemporalization, strategies that in referring to a timeless validity perpetuate classical ideas of order.

These detemporalization strategies fail when we move on to the level of *saying*, where time as spoken about swings back upon itself in the form of *time of speech*. More precisely, what is going on here is a *doubling of time* that corresponds to the doubling of instances of speech in Émile Benveniste (see 1966, Engl. 1968, ch. 20). "I promise you (now) that I *will* come tomorrow (on May 13)." Here two tenses appear: the now of the promising, and the datable later of what is promised. It is not at all the case that the act of promising appears earlier than the announced keeping of the promise — this would only hold for a report speaking about the promising. The reason why the act of promising does not appear earlier is that the act as such does not at all happen in time. Rather it opens up a time in which the speaker is obligated to do something or other. One might think of inaugural events, when legal contracts are concluded or constitutions given. The inaugural event takes place at a zero point, as Husserl calls it, that is not to be found as any given point within a system of co-ordinates (see below p. 103). A promise could not be repeated, a vow not be renewed, if it had passed away like a datable event occupying a place in a field of time or on a time line. Certain anniversaries lose their significance when all they keep alive is a historical reminiscence. In short, promising is not part of what is promised but rather signifies a *surplus of saying in what is said*, a surplus said along with what is said without coming up in this. Of course all this goes not only for acts of promising but also for threats, congratulations, and even for assertions. These too commit the speaker in such a way that taking them back means more than just a contrary assertion.

We touch upon a further level as soon as we confront saying with an *other saying*. This leads to a peculiar *time-lag*. The usual time-lag arises when we change over from one time system to another. At some point we adjust our watch; and at some point the inner, bodily or flesh clock adjusts as well. Yet time-lag in speech says more, namely that speech is shifted in relation to itself and does not exactly coincide with itself. We are never entirely at the top of time; rather we arrive upon the scene with a certain delay, and our speech reverberates against us like an echo of ourselves. Our speech would only be fully at home with itself if there were a first word without a before, a last word without an after. Only then could the word fully collect itself and overcome every dispersal. Our opening passage, borrowed from Jorge Semprun, indicates that this is not possible.

In the aporia of the first and last word we observe what Husserl goes through at the level of "primal impression." Removed from all traces of past, the primal impression would be an atom of sensation without any horizon. It could only be thought of as a point, as an "ideal limit" (Hua X, 40), but even such a basic thinking presupposes that something is experienced *as such*, based on an original repetition. We always come back to what we see when we see it as such. What appears only once does not appear at all (*einmal ist keinmal*). This would also hold for speech with no horizon. Only the unarticulated cry would remain as a limit case, the cry that tears the weave of speech and has no meaning; it at most hints at this meaning in pleasure or pain, in a sound close to falling silent.

Accordingly, time-lag means that speaking begins elsewhere, in the realm of a pre-language, a pre-predicative, a pre-discursive realm. The hyphen points to a threshold of experience, not to an unblemished ground of experience untouched by any language. Language is by no means everything, as some would have us think, but this is not because there is something else alongside it. It is rather because it precedes itself and oversteps itself, because in this sense it has itself a *Leib* or flesh[4] and does not just speak about that.

Time of the Senses

If there is to be an experience of time then time must in some way refer to the senses, thus to something that affects us, that is given to us, and waits for our response. But here begin new difficulties.

Can we assume a *perceived* time that we see, hear and touch, or that we at least see, hear, touch along *with* something else? Then we would be faced with the question of what we understand by perception, and to what extent time works its way into perception itself. If we restrict perception to a passive receiving or registering, then we only have to deal with physical data, with impressions or objects that are actually present in perception and accordingly may be reduced to the punctuality of the temporal moment without coming to terms with the elapsing of time. The transition to psychological time promises to save us, since the psyche is able to represent what is not present as well as what is not actual. It does this by arranging its own lived experiences in such a way that they follow each other in succession or stay together with one another at the same time, as opposed to the way spatial things stand out from one another. With this transition to a distension of the soul (*distentio animi*), to an intuition-form of the inner sense or to an unextended *durée* in Augustine, Kant, and Bergson, we encounter the oppositions already mentioned, where inner sense and with it time are privileged over outer sense and space. This privilege springs from an augmentation of the present. By collecting itself in itself and returning to itself from its dispersal, spirit approaches an omnipresence in which time is increasingly dispensed with. This privileging of the inner over and against the outer is expressed in the traditional hierarchic ordering of the arts, which rise from the lower levels of the plastic arts through the art of tone up to a pure art of words. This spiritualization entails a corresponding despatialization and detemporalization.

A revision that leaves behind the internalisation as well as the externalisation of time takes shape as soon as we proceed from the *embodiment of the senses.* Here the alternatives "passive givenness" and "active positing" lose their power. Perception, anchored in a fleshed here and now, is carried out as self-movement, as *kinaesthesia.* This traditional expression adopted by Husserl does not mean sensation of movement, but rather sensing that moves itself. In looking, listening, feeling, tasting, or sniffing, my body responds to that which comes to the fore, occurs to me, surprises me and affects me in the flesh of my body. In perception the world is staged and not simply registered in its details. Time is already involved in this in many ways, for example in the time of the gaze (*des Blicks*), in the glimpse of a moment (*Augen-blick*), which approximates the time of speech already mentioned. The gaze, which receives its motive impulse from elsewhere, precedes itself and comes back to itself in the form of a glimpse ahead and back (*eines Vor- und Rückblicks*). In his *Phenomenology of Perception* (p. 276 f., Engl. p. 239) Merleau-Ponty describes in vivid colours the temporality of seeing:

> For us the perceptual synthesis is a temporal synthesis, and subjectivity, at the level of perception, is nothing but temporality, and this is what enables us to leave to the subject of perception his opacity and historicity. I open my eyes on to my table, and my consciousness is flooded with colours and confused reflections; it is hardly distinguishable from what is offered to it; it spreads out, through its accompanying body, into the spectacle which so far is not a spectacle of anything. Suddenly, I start to focus my eyes on the table which is not yet there, I begin to look into the distance while there is as yet no depth, my body centres itself on an object which is still only potential, and so disposes its sensitive surfaces as to make it a present reality. I can thus re-assign to its place in the world the something which was impinging upon me, because I can, by slipping into the future, throw into the immediate past the world's first attack upon my senses, and direct myself towards the determinate object as towards a near future. The act of looking is indivisibly prospective, since the object is the final stage of my process of focusing, and retrospective, since it will present itself as preceding its own appearance, as the "stimulus," the motive or the prime mover of every process since its beginning. The spatial synthesis and the synthesis of the object are based on this unfolding of time.

The temporality of the senses may be illuminated from yet another perspective, namely by proceeding from the movement form *rhythm.*[5] Rhythm, in its original etymological sense a kind of flowing, designates since Plato the ordering of movement (τάξις τῆς κινήσεως) that gives form and measure to movement (*Laws* 664 e–665 a). This continues in Aristotle when in the *Physics* (IV, 11, 219 b 2) he determines time as the "number of motion with respect to 'before' and 'after'." The counting in question here presupposes countable, discrete units, and rhythm fulfils just this function of an articulation of movement. Rhythm accounts for the *return of the same*, which is measured out in beats. If all things were to remain the same, to flow into one another, and if nothing stood out in contrast to something else, then there would be no rhythm. One would always be stepping into the same river and even this sameness would have nothing from which it could stand out. In this sense rhythm takes on an elementary function of supporting order. Rhythm enjoys particular attention in the sphere of periodically and cyclically returning life processes, and in the sphere of acoustic art, which as melody and rhythm goes as far as the sound of words. Gestalt theory ultimately extended forms of movement to all the senses. Such forms are neither purely physical nor purely psychical; the formation of forms is played out between things and our body and reaches beyond both of these, as in the case of a rhythmically varying motor activity of colour vision, analysed by Kurt Goldstein (1934, pp. 167–174). Valéry concludes from this: "It is impossible to *think* a *rhythm*." He illustrates this claim with an experiment: "Hold still and try to represent a rhythm. Impossible. I knew someone who believed that he could do this and kept the beat with his eyelids. Or with twitches in the muscles of his mouth" (*Les Cahiers*, vol. I, p. 1340).

But this goes beyond the straightforward return. The return of the same presents itself at the same time as the *return of what is not the same*. What is initially decisive in this is that as the articulation of time's moving on, rhythm produces order and alters it. If we attend to the genesis of order, rather than grounding ourselves in an already completed order, then rhythm means not only "There is something *that* repeats itself"; it also means "There is something only *in* the fact that it repeats itself" This is how we come to see an order coming to be (*entstehende*) behind the existing (*bestehende*) order. Something *is* not identical, but *becomes* identical; it becomes identified in the fact that our experience continually comes back to something as something (Hua I, § 18). Repetition *makes the same of what is not the same*. In this sense repetition means an altering repetition, a return as the same of what is not the same. In contrast to what Plato says (*Rep.* 400 c–d), rhythm never rises to a pure eurhythmy, but is instead always interspersed with moments of arrhythmia.

Modern music which — like modern art in general — moves in different ways along the limits of order, operates not only with syncopes that disrupt the beat but also with counter-rhythms or overlapping rhythms, which release a heterophony. The rhythm of the senses ultimately emerges in language as well, in fact at the level of a pre-language that moves just this side of the meaning threshold although it always brushes against it. For something to be able to return *as something*, there must always already be *something* that returns. Accordingly, language acquisition begins with the pre-semantic recognising of phonic forms and written images. Hearing speech and seeing writing always extends into speaking and writing, with its meaning projections and validity claims. The rhythmic at work here leads to an open formation of meaning and of self that goes through the senses. This "sense [*Sinn*] of the senses" always has a temporal aspect.

Time of Forgetting and Remembering

In forgetting and remembering we immediately encounter the powerful effectiveness of time and not only its order. Here forgetting gains priority: without forgetting there is no remembering. Forgetting is an unwieldy phenomenon; it does not fit into the current schemata of meaning and validity. Forgetting concerns us, but it cannot be understood as an intentional act or rule-governed comportment. It has neither a meaning upon which we are intent, nor is it subject to a rule that is ours to follow; and yet it means more than an erasing of traces that merely prevents any effect. Forgetting belongs to all that happens to us, that befalls us like an accident. It has a peculiar sense of "in between." What is forgotten does not coincide with past facts which cannot be undone. Forgetting is not freely at our disposal, and yet it unsettles us. It may be described merely as a loss — loss of a knowing, an ability, or a feeling — or as a darkening, withdrawal. To the extent that it unsettles us, the forgotten is there and not there; it comes close to what Freud describes as repression.

Yet not every forgetting disconcerts us. One may distinguish different grades of forgetting to which different levels of past correspond. There is the *normal forgetting* of what was once available. This concerns a kind of unlearning in which learning is undone. What made an impression on us loses its striking character. To be distinguished from this is a *prior forgetting* (*Vorvergessen*) of that which was never consciously lived through or even planned. These are things such as one's own childhood, dreams, states of intoxication and delusion, or the holes in memory that swirl around like a whirlpool from which we can never fully extricate ourselves. Finally, there is in the background a *primal forgetting* (*Urvergessen*) in which the prior forgetting reaches its outermost limit, as in the case of birth where, according to Plato, we drink from the river Lethe. Expressed less mythically, this constitutes an "originary past that was never present" (Merleau-Ponty 1945, p. 280, Engl. p. 242). The originary forgetting manifests itself as an originary, irrevocable form of delay that determines our existence through and through and gives it the temporal index of an "a priori perfect" as Heidegger puts it in *Sein und Zeit* (p. 85, Engl. p. 117). This irrevocable delay repeats itself in all decisive occurrences, the effect of which precedes our registration or interpretation of them, our coping with them. It repeats itself with particular intensity in the posteriority or the belated effects of those traumatic experiences that shackle us to the past.

There is a further question concerning the location of forgetting. Like all experience, forgetting also takes place in the present. It breaks into experience like an accident, a lapse, as in Plato. Forgetting approximates those *Einfälle* and *Auffälligkeiten* i.e. those surprising things that occur to us, that strike us, in that they happen to me, befall me. I am involved in forgetting, but in the dative of giving and taking, not in the nominative of a named perpetrator. Forgetting would not especially unsettle us if the present enclosed us like a mussel. But a closed present only comes to be through the shielding that in an extreme case erects a bulwark to protect us from the past breaking in. When, on the other hand, we assume with Husserl that every present perception crosses over into retention, this means that when we retain something we are looking for a hold that we cannot find in the present. Forgetting does not begin at just any time and any place; it begins here and now. *We retain what threatens to slip out of our hands or our minds,* what we do not have firmly "in our grasp" (see Hua III, § 122). Because forgetting does not break into a secure enclosure of consciousness from the outside, it occurs as nearly total failure only in the limit case of fainting or the effect of shock. The gradual erosion triggered by forgetting presents itself as dedifferentiation, as deformation, as loss of relief (see Merleau-Ponty

1964b, p. 250, Engl. p. 197). Once again, forgetting points to the peculiarity of our body. Only he or she who is not fully "in" consciousness can forget. The simultaneity of self-reference and self-withdrawal that makes up consciousness explains why time effects, why it changes us, why we undergo it before we mesh with it. As "guards of the past," as Proust puts it in the first pages of his *Recherche*, the limbs of our body are only a vanguard of consciousness; they are not underlings there to carry out a guardian role.

Remembering, just as much as forgetting, does not begin with an act — for instance with an act of observation or with a new programming. Something occurs *to me* again in a similar way as something occurs *to me* at all, it returns into my mind just as it came into my mind. Remembering is awakened, not made. In this the alien comes into play, that which does not stem from our own initiative. Recollecting, which may be neither forced nor summoned under order does not, any more than does forgetting, present itself as an intentionally directed act or rule-governed comportment. Recollecting begins as taking up again, as putting on again, as *reprise*, as an ἀναλαμβάνειν, as it is called in the Platonic texts on Anamnesis. More recent attempts to replace the old storage model of memory with constructs and to turn remembering into a pure observer's category (J. Schmidt 1991, preface) entirely miss the experience of time, from which even the "builder" of constructs is not free. The simple reversal: "It is not memories that come from the past but rather the past that results from memories" (ibid., p. 34) signifies no more and no less than a philosophy of presence in constructivist clothing. Reservations emerge equally with regard to the reduction of forgetting to a not being able to remember, a reduction that equates forgetting with lacking competence and limited capacity. This technical domestication of time does not even allow for the question of whether something is worth remembering, whether it could validate a claim to memory. Neglecting the experience of time has the consequence that the technology of memory and the moralistic view of remembering largely run alongside one another, as if remembering were a mixture of storage capacity, developmental programming and good will. This renders the penetration of the past, the obsession with something past, totally harmless.[6]

Time of the Other

The temporal shifting we have already encountered in our own speech grows stronger when we consider how proper and alien speech interpenetrate one another. Here temporality gains a further dimension. The social character of time comes to the fore, that which makes us speak of contemporaries, of ancestors and of descendants. The commemoration of remembering already falls into this new dimension. It is in this context that Levinas opposes to the synchrony of meaning a *dia-chrony* that lifts the classical dia-logue off the hinges of a unified logos.[7] Even in classical dialogue, as this is presented to us in all its glory from Plato to Gadamer, there is definitely a time-lag, since the giving and taking of the words alternate. Yet this time-lag is only a relative one, a temporary movement within a continual occurrence of meaning. The here and now is co-ordinated and synchronised with respect to one and the same "thing [*Sache*] itself," which reveals itself in different aspect and perspectives; or it is played down with respect to validity claims to be tested by arguments. The reciprocity of perspectives according to Alfred Schütz, the reversibility of standpoints according to Jean Piaget,[8] both insure that my own and the Other's voice, my own and the Other's look, forfeit their alienness within a dialectic of sameness and otherness. This continues in the classical conception of history as world history, which mediates the proper (*Eigenes*) and the alien (*Fremdes*) in a collective work. What counts is the net yield. A universal-pragmatic normalisation of reason, along the lines of Jürgen Habermas' ethics of discourse, changes nothing about the fact that the alien demand becomes neutralised.

As opposed to this, diachrony means that between the *Other's demand* and *my own response*, between the Other's and own speech, there is a gaping hiatus that interrupts the common flux of speech. The dash, which separates demand and response from one another, may not be turned into a hyphen. The alien demand signifies an *originary previousness* that is not to be anticipated from the present, whereas the proper response appears with an equally *originary posteriority* quality not to be overcome within the present. In this sense the response, which begins elsewhere, always has something traumatic about it. What is inscribed within experience, carved into it, does not freely unfold like a budding bloom. The entwined *Incipit* of modern novels also conveys something of the suffering from beginning, from the pain of remembering, that in Socratic maieutics is compared not without reason to labour pains. The oft-cited πάθοςμάθος means more than the pragmatic building of character through hardship or a method of trial and error. It means that every learning bears in itself the traces of an enduring, of something alien that may not be unlearned.

Synchrony, which amounts to a unified chronology, suffices only as long as the exchange of thoughts and wills remains within an order. It loses its synthetic power where the limits of order are transgressed. Where something *comes to language* that is not previously *found in it* we run up against something *unexpected.* There are breaches in time that make our experience of time fall apart into heterochronies.[9] Time thresholds, which we never leave behind, make it possible and require that one not only needs time but also gives time; that one even gives what one does not already have; that there be something that is not already on stable ground.

All in all we live temporally, just as we exist in the flesh of our body. There is no timeless or bodiless outside, although the occurrence of time itself is interspersed with delays, postponements, with *ritardandi* of every kind. Time differentiates itself; it condenses into the present yet does not culminate in it. The consequence of this inner differentiation is that we find ourselves here and now and at the same time elsewhere and at some other time. This is where the split with other times continually opens: not a *nunc stans*, but a *nunc distans.*[10]

Lecture V

Bodily Experience between Selfhood and Otherness

Opening: *Loss of the face.* — In his novel *The Face of Another*[1] the Japanese novelist Kobo Abe tells us the story of a scientist whose face had been deformed, literally defaced by a laboratory accident. He learned to hide the "keloid scars, swollen and distended, red and black intertwining" (p. 12 f.), behind bandages and at last behind a plastic mask. First he tried to normalise what had happened to him and to overcome the shame he felt with arguments like these: "I can hardly believe that the face is so important to a man's existence. A man's worth should be gauged by the content of his work; possibly the convolutions of the surface of the brain have nothing to do with it, but his face certainly does not. If the loss of a face can cause conspicuous change in the scale of evaluation, it may well be owing to a fundamental emptiness of content." He tried to deceive himself about the loss by referring to the cultural habit of wearing clothes and masks: "If covering our bodies with clothes represents a cultural step forward, there is no guarantee that in the future masks will not be taken equally for granted. Even now they are often used in important ceremonies and festivals. I do not quite know how to put it, but I wonder if a mask, being universal, enhances our relations with others more than does the naked face." However, the story does not end here. In the end the injured man discovers through the eyes of his work associates, of the landlord of his flat and finally through the eyes of his wife what he has lost: a *tolerable look.* The phenomenon of the mask raises important questions concerning the protection of our face, but also concerning the roles we all play in our life or the roles of the actor, exhibited by the mask (*persona*) through which the voice sounds. We know so many tricks to make up our face and to cultivate our image. We can see to what extent we are ourselves embodied and also embarrassed by the face, oscillating between familiarity and bewilderment. Someone who loses his or her face loses him- or herself, at least to some extent.

* * *

The Riddle of Our Body

Before philosophers try to define the status of our body, we are already familiar with it. The body is involved in our being in the world and in our being in the world with others. Nevertheless, from the very beginning there seems to be something strange about it. Our representations of the body are permeated by *mythical* and *religious* interpretations which are attached to the riddle of birth and death, to the soul's dream wanderings, to the ups and downs of our bodily forces and to the plague of sickness. The adventures of bodily life are pictured by outbursts of our imagination, such as by taking patterns from strong totem animals, by believing in the metempsychosis or the re-incarnation of the soul in other bodies, or by expecting the resurrection of the body. *Medical* research and treatment has always been and is still the main source for our concrete knowledge about the functioning body, including certain body schemes and body maps which leave space for corporeal centres, main roads and side roads. The impact of medical knowledge is due to the fact that our body makes itself felt particularly when its normal functions are disturbed or hampered. A lot of our bodily knowledge is a sort of alarm knowledge. Furthermore, our bodily behaviour includes an original kind of *somato-technique.* We do not only live in our body, we use it as a primary instrument. Thus we make use of our hand which, because of its flexibility, Aristotle calls the "organ of all organs," and this bodily achievement is extended and reinforced by the continuous invention of implements.[2] Our body appears as an interdisciplinary issue par excellence.

The multiplicity of our body's mode of being finds its echo in certain ambiguities of our common *language.* Most Western languages have only one word to signify human or animal bodies on the one hand, and natural bodies like stars, atoms or blood-corpuscles on the other hand (see σῶμα, *corpus, corps* or *body*).[3]

Consequently, philosophers have to specify the body by distinctions such as *corps vivant, corps propre* or *corps sujet* in opposition to *corps-chose* or *corps objet*, and these distinctions are often rather problematic. As older German authors like Feuerbach, Schopenhauer and Nietzsche have already noted, German allows us to distinguish between *Leib* (see the common phrase *Leib und Leben*) and *Körper*, which may be human or not. In order to exclude certain ambiguities which persist even in German, Husserl contrasts the functioning body (*fungierender Leib*) with the mere body (*Körper*) or the body as thing (*Körperding*).[4] In addition to this he sometimes uses the word *Leibkörper* in order to suggest that even our living body keeps some aspects of a physical entity. In what follows I shall make use of these distinctions in various ways. Moreover, in Husserl's view the bodily character of beings is over-determined. Thus, he qualifies the presence of things, which so to speak appear in person, as a sort of *leibhaftige Gegenwart.* Merleau-Ponty later used this linguistic hint as a bridge towards the elementary texture of the flesh (*chair*), which he ascribes to our own and to the Other's body as well as to language, time and Being.

But let us turn to the philosophy of the body in the Western tradition. It seems difficult to deny that philosophy is subject to an almost ineradicable dualist trend. The body is spontaneously understood not as a sphere of meditation, but as a contrast to something else. Body and soul, body and mind or spirit, or — transposed to the life of language — letter and spirit are all well-known oppositions. Whoever dares to speak of the body is expected to speak of something else *in addition.* When Nietzsche declares: "I am body through and through and nothing else" (*Leib bin ich ganz und gar und nichts sonst*)[5] he takes recourse to provocative expressions, eager to challenge certain Western prejudices. Who will deny that our classical thinking, inherited from the Greeks, has a certain congenital defect due to a devaluation of the body? Admittedly Plato was not a simple "despiser of the body." He defined dying and even philosophising as the separation of the soul from the body, but most of what concerns our senses and our body is sublimated and not simply repressed. In the *Timaios* even the cosmos, taken as a great living being, has a body and not only a soul. Nevertheless there remains the fact that somatic phenomena are put on an inferior level of the ontological and psychological hierarchy.

Later, Aristotle tried to bridge the gap between soul and body by conceiving the soul as the form (μορφή) of the material body. That makes a great difference, but even in his view the Spirit (νοῦς) comes from outdoors (θύραθεν) — not as a guest, but as the leader of everything.

If we now turn to the modern era, which is far from over, the more or less flexible cosmic hierarchy established between spirit or soul and body yields to a sharp sort of dualism which has no equal in classical cosmology and psychology. As happens so often, discovering and covering go hand in hand, such as in the case of Galileo to whom Husserl ascribes "a discovering and a covering (or concealing) genius" (*Crisis*, Hua VI, 53, Engl. 52). Indeed the destiny of the modern era is deeply marked by the fact that the mathematization of nature and the enthronement of the ego arose together and reinforce each other. Due to this two-fold process, everything that pertains to our bodily existence is twice overshadowed — by an autonomous subject and by a calculable nature. There is no better evidence of this than Descartes' thought. In Descartes' view it is me, the thinking ego, who refers to things; one of these things turns out to be myself as a *res cogitans*, some of them appear as others who think as I do, and most of them are merely physical examples of *res extensa.* But there remains the double problem of how to justify the fact that a certain physical body is called my own body (*corpus meum*) and how to find out whether there are other bodies that are animated by other minds. The irony of the story is that our body is also simultaneously covered and discovered. Our body appears as something split off from ourselves, although it belongs to us to some extent, at least when we suffer from it.

This dualistic conception is shaken by a first revision based on sense experience and linguistic expressions. It is admitted that it is indeed me who refers to things, to myself and to others, but added that I do so only by means of my body, which is permanently involved. No manipulation without hands, no communication without mouth and ears, no feeling without blood pressure and heartbeat, and so on. But this process of concretization stops half way. It is still presupposed that there is somebody or something which is *in*corporated and *em*bodied without being body through and through. So in the end, as a member of a spirit which pervades everything, I may return to myself and simultaneously reach the totality of beings by internalising what initially belonged to the exteriority of the body. I start from myself, but I end with an all-encompassing universe. It is not easy to say who gets farther from the truth of the body: Descartes who takes the *dualistic* part, insisting on a gap between mind and body, or Hegel who takes the *monistic* part, integrating the body into the totality of spirit. Traces of these old debates can still be found today even in the domain of the human sciences. On the one hand, even in the field of neurophysiology the distinction between the first- and third-person perspective is insisted upon. However, notwithstanding the utility of this distinction on the methodological and experimental level, the question remains open as to how to determine the X which is supposed to appear under two different perspectives. On the other hand every kind of monism, whether physical or biological, gets into trouble when confronted with beings which are not only spoken about or seen by us, but for their own part speak to us and look at us.

However there is another kind of revision which reaches deeper than this half-Cartesian or simply anti-Cartesian skirmish. Is it not true that in a certain sense I *am* my body and you *are* your body, as some phenomenologists claim? Do I only *have* pains or perceptions as if I were the owner of my experience? If we assume, as Helmuth Plessner does, that *being* my body and *having* it are closely connected,[6] we are faced with a difference and with other kinds of fissures which pertain to the sphere of our body, constituting its very being and not destroying it. Our *bodily* experience would by far exceed the experience *of the body*. In a way similar to how, in Husserl's view, our experience of time presupposes the temporality of experience itself, the experience of our body would presuppose the corporeality of experience itself. Nietzsche, the most important forerunner of the phenomenology of the body, extolled the body as "great reason" or as a self which *dwells* in your body as a "mighty sovereign" and an "unknown wise man," which even *is* your body.[7] But if this is true we are invited to enter the labyrinth of the body and find out how the power of this sovereign devolves upon the different members of the body and how the unknown wisdom of the body works. The *Philosophie am Leitfaden des Leibes*, which the later Nietzsche looked forward to (see his Posthumous Fragments from the eighties), has to spell the old words "object," "subject" and "intersubjectivity," *logos* and *pathos*, in a new way. That does not mean that we simply return to the traditional order, trying to replace the modern *natura*, fraught with all its fissures and splits, as if we were habitants of an intact sphere of Being.

In what follows I want to tackle this task, making reference to the three phenomenological issues of intentionality, of self-awareness and of intersubjectivity, showing how all that can be translated from the traditional language of consciousness into a new language of bodily experience. Considering that this is a huge task it will have to suffice to mark only a few crucial points. I shall select those which are especially important for my own research and which may also be important for others who are working in the same field.

Intentionality and Affection

One could say that intentionality is the shibboleth of phenomenology, just as for Freud unconsciousness was the shibboleth of psychoanalysis. But in both cases the key word is far from being the last word. It does not solve the riddle, instead it opens an immense field of questions.

What does it mean to claim that something is intended? To put it in simple terms, it means that something is given, apprehended, understood or interpreted *as something* i.e. endowed with a certain sense. In this respect, together with hermeneutics and analytical philosophy, phenomenology belongs to a larger family which may be termed the philosophy of sense. Traditional distinctions such as outer vs. inner world, physical vs. mental entities, real conditions vs. ideal rules are overcome by this tiny word *as*, *als*, *comme*, ᾗ or *qua* which functions as a sort of joint, connecting the disconnected. Nothing is given which is not given *as such* e.g. as a red blood stain, as the taste of strawberry, as Pegasus or dragons flying, as a love letter, as a hammer or sword, as a symptom of illness, as a spectrogram, as a terrorist attack or an act of liberation and so on, and nobody is involved in such experiences without behaving *as somebody*, always playing a certain role. As phenomenologists we refuse to separate what something is or who somebody is from how it is given and how we get access to it. The How of givenness and of accessibility pertains to the things themselves. Further, what appears as something or as somebody appears *in this way rather than in another*. Therefore every sense is a preferred one without being the true sense, and every sense is tainted with contingency. Finally, what appears as such again and again is in itself marked as repeatable. Ideality or rationality are not imposed on raw data, rather they originate from experience itself, before being represented in terms of intuitive ideas or explicit rules. Such a theory of sense, based on a "logos of the aesthetic world" (Hua XVII, 297), resists the temptation of doubling the real world with an ideal "after-world." There is only this one world i.e. the world from which we start even when we keep our distance from what our eyes see and what our ears hear, and even when we imagine other worlds or enter virtual spaces.

What does all this have to do with our body? Certainly, our body participates in the work of experience in many ways, but nevertheless it seems not to be the author of all these *intentional acts* which are ascribed to consciousness, including the consciousness of our body. Plato already claimed that it is not our eyes that see, but rather that it is our soul which sees by means of the eyes. However the alternative "we or the eyes" may be a false alternative. Let us turn again to the formula *something as something.* What about the *something* which is taken as something? Initially, Husserl makes use of Aristotelian language, speaking of a certain *hyle* i.e. something *out of which* something is formed by intentional acts. This may be true on a certain level of normality where things *are* what they are and are known as such. Here we may distinguish the repeatable form from the various materials by which it is realised, just as Aristotle does when referring to tables or houses. But things look rather different when we get to the roots of experience where things *become* what they could be.[8] Let us take the case of perception. Perceiving does not start with an act of observation. On the contrary, it arises with an event of attention which is aroused and provoked by what strikes me, *was mir auffällt.* Or let us take the case of actions. They start from situations which offer something which attracts or repels us, which looks frightening or tempting. Our actions are, as Husserl himself concedes, more staged than produced (cf. Hua IV, 98, 259, 336), running through phases of hesitation and rehearsals. Memory functions in a similar way. As Nietzsche puts it, we only keep in mind what hurts us. And our spontaneous memory, meticulously described by Bergson and Proust, follows our desires and not our will. In a certain sense we are overcome by our past before taking it up. Finally, even our thinking starts from ideas which occur to us, from what in

German is called *Einfälle*, what Lacan, referring to the irruption of the significant, renders as *incidences* (Écrits, p. 515).

In sum, everything that appears as something has to be described not simply as something which receives a sense, but as something which provokes sense without being meaningful itself yet still as something *by which* we are touched, affected, stimulated, surprised and to some extent violated. I call this happening pathos, *Widerfahrnis* or af-fect, marked by a hyphen in order to suggest that something is done *to us*. In German the prefix *an-* allows for a series of verbs such as *Angehen, Anblicken, Anreden* or just *Antun*, and Husserl latterly also follows these linguistic hints when developing his theory of affection.[9] One may doubt whether he goes far enough in order to draw the due conclusions. In any case, behind intentional acts, ascribed to a subject as their author or source, there appear events that we undergo, something which happens to us. Those events belong neither to a first-person perspective as an act I perform, nor to the third-person perspective as an objective process registered or effected from the outside. They require a language in which the *id* or *Es* is entangled with a *me* or *to me*, a *mich* or *mir*. In this respect the ego, appearing in the accusative or the dative, precedes the ego in the nominative. From the very beginning I am involved, but not under the title of a responsible author or agent. I have suggested using the term *patient* in its literal sense in order to underline this passive pre-status of the so-called subject. The corresponding status would be that of a *respondent* who re-sponds to what strikes him or her. The *Wodurch*, i.e. something that we are affected by, appears as such only in terms of a *Worauf*, i.e. of something to which we respond. The *Nachträglichkeit*, the posteriority of the response we are invited to give corresponds to the *Vorgängkeit*, the previousness of the pathos we undergo. So in everything we do we are separated from our own origin by a genuine form of time-lag (see Lecture IV). Without such a radical form of temporality, which connects what it separates and separates what it connects, the motive of passivity would loose its force. It would be either located inside as the subject's own limit, e.g. as the signature of its finitude, or outside as reality's raw remnant, e.g. as uncoded stimulus.

Again raising the question of our body's role we see that this question has already been answered in part. Being affected by and exposed to what is alien to myself (*Ichfremdes*) depends neither on our knowing nor on our willing i.e. on our consciousness, it is related to our body. The domain of our body includes all that really has to do with me without being done by me. In this regard the body which Merleau-Ponty once called an "inborn complex" (1945, p. 99, Engl. p. 84) comes close to the unconscious, to the corporeal ego (*Körper-Ich*) and to the corporeal language of symptoms in Freud's psychoanalysis. Take also the case of aphonia, presented by Ludwig Binswanger and extensively commented on by Merleau-Ponty (ibid., pp. 187–193, Engl. pp. 160–166): a girl looses her language in reaction to her mother's prohibition of her seeing her beloved. But crossing the borderline between phenomenology and psychoanalysis would be a far-reaching endeavour.[10] In this context it may be sufficient to emphasise what we can call the *birth of sense out of pathos*; like any other sort of birth it is not free of labour. Besides, our body seems to be more human than a mind that merely functions. Therefore we should not only ask what a computer can or cannot do, but what does and what does not happen to it, what it responds to and what it does not respond to.

The Split Self

Whereas intentionality governs our exchange with the world, the search for self-consciousness or self-awareness confronts us with ourselves. Once more we are faced with the question of how this self-reference appears when regarded from the standpoint of our body. In contrast to earlier forms of self-reference such as care for oneself, the modern access to ourselves is largely assigned to what is called reflection. But the use of this concept, borrowed from optics, is full of pitfalls. Locke's attempt to take the self as something *beside* things, complementing outer experience with an inner one, seems strictly excluded when we work on the basis of intentionality. If I am somebody by whose intentional acts things are constituted as such, and somebody to whom they are given, the ego cannot be reduced to a mere "tag-end of the world" (*Endchen der Welt*) (Hua I, 63). I am involved in whatever may appear. Thus for Husserl reflection does not mean a sort of inner experience, but transcendental reflection i.e. the thematization of the correlation between meaning and act and of my living in the world. In other words, reflection transforms functioning intentionality into an explicit intentionality. It is obvious that this reflection displays many corporeal aspects. We see, hear, touch ourselves and move by ourselves. So our own corporeality "refers to itself" in its own activity (Hua I, 128). This self-referential activity includes different forms of self-affection. When looking into a looking-glass, hearing our voice on the tape or touching a sharp knife we surprise ourselves, we are captured by our image, bewildered by our own voice or we simply cut into our own flesh. But as long as we interpret this being for oneself as "being intentionally related to oneself" (Hua I, 81) we step onto an endless path of iteration. We fly from one reflection to the next without approaching what we are reflecting on. We may learn from this Sisyphus-like activity that the bodily self is a *Nicht-Ding* (a non-thing), never "bodily present (*leibhaft gegenwärtig*)" as things are. The chain of reflections hangs on a pre-reflective nucleus of vivid presence which can only be grasped afterwards by a sort of "after-awareness (*Nachgewahren*)" (Hua VIII, 89). So we may infer that self-reference was nothing more than a lack of reference to things, just as our body appears as a "strangely imperfectly constituted thing" when compared to ordinary things (Hua IV, 159). Long-standing discussions revolving around self-consciousness have demonstrated *usque ad nauseam* that every attempt to constitute self-consciousness by reflection presupposes the self it is looking for. Even so-called auto-poiesis i.e. self-fabrication is not free from such difficulties.

But there are other problems which are much closer to our issue of the body. Obviously we are acquainted with numerous processes and states which pertain to our body such as blood pressure, hormone balance, firing of neurones, or last but not least the functioning of "my brain" as the central part of "my body." But does all this participate in the above-mentioned forms of sensory reflections? Obviously not. It makes no sense to declare that our brain reflects on itself as if it were the successor of the ancient homunculus. When neurologists admit that the brain selects or evaluates certain stimuli, they are really referring to operations which do not need an operative self. Recursive processes, produced by operative loops, are rather different from reflective acts. One may try to cope with this incursion of physics into the sphere of our living body by remitting the whole neuro-physiological apparatus to a naturalistic attitude so that the so-called personalistic attitude seems to remain intact. Nothing more would be left than mere *correlations* between neuro-physiological processes on the one hand, psychological or mental acts and states on the other hand. But we will not get rid of the soul-body problem by means of such a clear-cut distinction. Certainly, the brain as brain is a neurological construct, but what we may call the "functioning brain" is not a mere construct, it belongs to our living or functioning body and not to some physical annex. The simple distinction between two attitudes which Husserl offers in the second volume of his *Ideas* (Hua IV) is still too closely connected with the presumed consciousness of our body, and so it leads us back on to the Cartesian track. It sounds much more convincing when Husserl qualifies the body as the "transfer-point (*Umschlagstelle*)" between sense and natural causality (Hua IV, 286). Technology, which includes various, ever increasing technologies of the body, confronts us with further problems which call for a genuine form of phenomenotechnics. This can be shown by simple examples taken from our body's everyday life. When I hear my voice on a tape or see my face on a video I get into a situation where nearness and remoteness are entangled and where all direct reflection is disturbed by a sort of deflection. Old photo albums in which I encounter my childhood show who I was and who I could have been, and like Robert Musil's "Man without Qualities" we may ask what binder would be strong enough to prevent us from splitting into pieces (1978, p. 648).

These are real problems, and it may be tempting to leave them behind by taking refuge in a pure self, a pure feeling of our body, an immanence of life, a sort of self-affection which precedes all that thrusts us outside ourselves: the whirl of temporality, the ecstasies of intentionality and the challenge by others. But such a bodily narcissism is based on untenable premises. To take the body *as body* always presupposes a certain distance from one's own body, which Plessner calls "eccentric positionality" (1981, pp. 360–365; 1983, pp. 190–195). The pure body, or to put it in German, a *Leib* without *Körper*, belongs to the periphery of Cartesianism: *sentio, ergo sum.* But becoming aware of what one feels and giving it some expression means more than merely feeling it.

So we have to look for other ways out. Insisting on a split self may be such a way. Once more Descartes will help us to clear up what is at stake here. His position cannot be simply skipped, it has to be taken into account and transformed. Otherwise it will return again and again. In the Cartesian view there are two modes of being: thinking minds and extended things. Using the language of visibility we can approach the problem in the following way: minds are seeing, but not seen, things are seen, but not seeing. By contrast, our body does not fit into this dualistic scheme. First, our body is exactly both these at once: seeing and seen, hearing and heard, touching and touched, moving and moved. Secondly, the one who sees and what is seen never coincide as *cogito* and *cogitatum* are supposed to. This non-coincidence cannot be understood as a deficit, it characterises the very being of our body, which refers to itself and at the same time evades itself. Our first example of sensuous reflection should not be taken as an esthesiological version of the Aristotelian νόησις νοήσεως, as a kind of ὅρασις ὁράσεως introduced by Plotinus (*Enn.* V, 3, 8). What escapes my own eyes is not *something* or *somebody* seen, but the very *event of becoming visible.* Something strikes me and catches my eye (*fällt mir ins Auge*). It is my own gaze which withdraws, not my eyes as body organs which I can indeed observe in the mirror and with the shape or colours of which I can identify. The gaze which responds to what appears has no colour. To this extent it must be qualified as invisible. When I assume that the mirror image is reversed, I refer to myself as if I were looking at myself and not to myself as simply reflected on a smooth surface, because in that case the reflections would be simply in their place. If this self-withdrawal is compared with the blind spot on the retina, we must take care not to confuse the invisible reversal of the visible with a mere lacunae within the field of vision.

Our body appears not only as visible, but also as audible, touchable, movable or as an expressive and libidinous body. The splitting of my own body spreads out in different directions. Thus in Ovid the young Narcissus who falls in love with himself and falls to his death by becoming immersed in his own mirror image is haunted by the nymph Echo, who is only able to react and to repeat what has been said. This rendezvous which fails twice teaches us a lot about our bodily condition. The echo appears as the acoustic counterpart of the looking-glass effect. We hear ourselves speak although we are the ones who speak. Verbal hallucinations, in which patients hear voices from the outside although they produce them themselves, would be completely incomprehensible if the voice were always my own voice in the fullest sense. Cartesians should wonder how to explain the fact that a thinking being is capable of hallucinating. Such patients would otherwise be degraded to strange animals, and psychiatry would lose, as has often been the case, its human face.

As to the moving body, it plays the role of a *basso continuo* for all kinds of action. This is an old issue. In Aristotle's view the self is moved by goals which attract or repel our striving. Detached from emotions, reason moves nothing. In modern times the movement of the body also suffers from the dualistic view. In his treatise *Passiones animae* Descartes draws a clear distinction between action where I move something from inside, and passion where I am moved from outside. Moving or being moved, or to put it in Kantian terms causality of freedom or causality of nature, is the crucial question. But if it is true that our practical behaviour as well as other forms of behaviour start with being affected and continue by responding, we must admit that we are self-moving. We participate and intervene in a motion which is already on the road and which precedes our initiative. Every player of a musical instrument knows that his or her fingers are quicker and more sensitive than any rational control could be. If we imagine a Chinese person who writes down the eleven strokes for "elephant" (象) or the seventeen strokes for "flute" (籥), shying at each new stroke like a horse at the water-jump, writing would be a long story.[11] We are carried away (*mitgerissen, emportés*) by our own words and actions as well as by those of others, so that we are neither reduced to merely moved objects nor to simply active subjects. That is why our every-day life is infiltrated by what Freud calls *Fehlleistungen*, by a sort of parapraxis which belongs to our praxis without being reducible to voluntary decisions. Being moved without moving and, vice versa, moving without being moved are only extreme borderline cases by which either we descend to the lower state of lifeless things or we ascend to the higher state of a godlike "first mover" who, according to Aristotle, moves by being loved without for his part loving (cf. *Met.* XII, 1072 b 3).

We could continue in this way and show that all our behaviour arises from a sort of self-affection which we undergo and respond to. We are older than ourselves and as a result of the fact of our birth and a further series of second births we are incapable of making up our *Selbstvorsprung*, our precedence to ourselves or lead-on to ourselves. The birth of sense out of pathos, mentioned above, finds its complement in the *birth of myself out of pathos.* My original delay or posteriority generates an irreducible sort of alienness which I have called *ecstatic alienness.* I get outside myself, not by chance, illness or weakness, but by being who I am. This alterity consists in a broken self-reference i.e. in a sort of self-reference which includes special forms of self-withdrawal. Connected with myself and at the same time cut off from myself, I am neither simply one nor simply two, but two in one and one in two. The inner tension between both poles leaves room for extreme forms of confusion and dismemberment. Monism and dualism find a certain truth in it.

Concerning the old problem of the relationship between soul and body, we could speak of a *Leibkörper* as Husserl, Scheler or Plessner used to do. This complex being includes not only the living body by and through which we perceive and manipulate things, by which and through which we express ourselves and collaborate with each other, but includes as well all the physiological apparatus, including neurological and genetic processes, by which our own behaviour is not only realised but to some extent shaped. All this belongs to us, but in terms of a decreasing nearness and an increasing remoteness. So I am justified in speaking of *my* brain. We must only take into consideration that belonging *to me* does not *eo ipso* mean being at my disposal, as if I were the owner of my body. We direct our eyes, we stretch out our hands or we speed up our steps, but we do not hold our breath or increase our blood pressure as if we were adjusting a computer programme. This does not exclude the fact that the so-called higher activities of thinking and willing and the aforementioned physiological processes interact with each other. Strong affects such as astonishment or anxiety which break into our normal life and provoke reactions are in general surrounded by a corporeal aura. If we take care not to submit thinking and speaking exclusively to mere standards of clearness or correctness, but on the contrary take into account deeper convictions and long-lasting habits, nothing prevents us from admitting an incarnate form of thinking which in German may be called *leibhaftig.* There is no thinking and willing without all kinds of belief and habit which are far from being at our free disposal. It was novelists such as Dostojevski who stressed that at night we believe in another way than in the daylight. And it was Nietzsche who complained that the ideas of philosophers tend too much to be acquired by "squatting" (*ersessen*) instead of being "walked" (*ergangen*). In German we call this

Gedankengänge (trains of thought). We should take Gassendi's *ambulo ergo sum* not as the reversal of Descartes' *cogito ergo sum*, but as its embodiment.

The continuous scale of nearness and remoteness leaves room for the most diverse forms of pathology. I would suggest cases of depersonalisation where the patient's hand lies on the table like a stone, or cases of schizophrenia where somebody is cut off from his own ideas, or cases of trauma where somebody is fixated on what happened to him or her but is unable to respond to it. However such pathological fissures do not fall completely outside the normal splitting of our self, which is always pervaded and haunted by certain anomalies. Over-normalisation itself leads to certain pathologies. Considered from the standpoint of the body, illness calls for corresponding forms of therapy which try to overcome the Cartesian division into somatic and mental disease. We can and should make other distinctions e.g. by distinguishing between forms of disease which remain on the periphery of the bodily self and other forms which touch the heart of our existence. When Pascal ascribed to the human being the paradoxical state of a "thinking reed" he came nearer to the truth of the body than did Descartes who only subsequently, on turning from the order of reason to the order of life, conceded a mixture of soul and body.

The Other as My Double

The alienness in the midst of myself opens paths to the alienness of the Other. It prevents us again from stumbling along the paths of traditional dualism. From that point of view there are some bodies which are to be called *other bodies* only in relationship to *other minds.*[12] Whenever I start from a consciousness of the Other (*Fremdbewußtsein*) the alienness of the Other will inevitably be constituted on the basis of my "sphere of ownness," "within and by means of that which is my own" (Hua I, 131, Engl. 100).[13] The otherness of the Other will always be derived from the own. The Other appears as an *alter ego* i.e. strictly as a second me. But as soon as we adopt the standpoint of the body and proceed from a bodily self which is "not master in its own house," the Other arises as co-original with myself and to some extent as earlier than myself. In order to avoid the traditional egocentrism based on a *subjectum* underlying everything and everybody we are confronted with, I follow Merleau-Ponty who changes intersubjectivity into *intercorporeity.* The exchange of the leading figure also changes the nature of the between; it changes the *inter* of the inter-change and inter-course which takes place between us.

When we now consider the status of the Other we encounter two aspects which seem to be especially important. First, the Other originally appears neither as *something* I transform into somebody by way of empathy or of argument by analogy, nor as *somebody* whose intentions I understand, interpret or share. On the contrary, the otherness or the alienness of the Other announces itself once more in terms of pathos, of a specific *Fremdaffektion.* We are touched by others before being able to ask who they are and what their behaviour or their utterances mean. The Other's otherness, which overcomes and surprises us, disturbs our intentions before being understood in this or that sense. The second aspect I want to emphasise is connected with the fact that I am not only affected by another ego or subject, i.e. by somebody different from myself, but by *meinesgleichen,* by *mon semblable,* by people like me who are, however, at the same time incomparable, *unvergleichlich, hors de série.* We should not take the entrance of the Other for granted as do so many theories of language, of society or culture. There are not only "miracles of reason," evoked by Leibniz[14] and taken up by Husserl and Merleau-Ponty, there is also a "miracle of the Other." We find apples, tables or computers, just like this one I have before my eyes or in my hands, but none of these things *has* something like itself as its equal. Being some*body* rather than only some*thing* simply implies having equals. These equals remain unequal because of their singularity, which is rooted in their incarnate being, in their being here and now. I call this strange fact which cannot be derived from anything else the *doubling of myself in and by the Other.* In this way my own ecstatic alienness is reinforced by the *duplicative alienness* of the Other. In this context I allude again to the motif of the double, the *Doppelgänger,* as I did in my lecture on events. Nobody has more strongly connected this motife with the existence of the Other than Paul Valéry. So I quote once more from his *Cahiers* (vol. I, p. 499), this time in full length: "The Other, the likes of me, or maybe my double, that is the most magnetic abyss — the most reviving question, the most malicious obstacle — something which alone prevents all that remains from being confused, from being altogether estranged. Rather ape than imitator — reflex which responds, precedes, amazes."[15]

This strange kind of otherness may be illustrated by the same examples we have already drawn upon in respect to my own alienness. The Other's gaze, to which I am exposed, consists in the fact that I feel myself seen before seeing the Other as somebody who sees things, including myself. The fact that I feel myself seen reaches its extreme in the paranoid delusion of observation (*Beobachtungswahn*). It cannot be reduced to the simple effect, admitted by system theorists, that I see what you do not see and that you see what I do not see. The "blind spot" inherent in the experience of the Other exceeds the mere limits of capacity attributed to self-referential systems, which are unable to include their own functioning. It makes no sense to claim that a machine feels persecuted by the sensors of other machines. The human Other does not only confront us with the limits of our own possibilities. The affection by the Other overcomes us as *wirkende Wirklichkeit,* as effective reality preceding the conditions of possibility analysed by transcendental philosophy and specified in terms of rule systems or codes. The experience of the Other is strictly speaking im-possible; it is not made possible in advance either by my own initiative or by general rules. Like Schelling we may call it immemorial (*unvordenklich*).

What holds true for the Other's gaze also characterises the Other's voice. I feel myself looked at or addressed prior to hearing somebody utter certain words or produce certain sounds. Being appealed to *by somebody* and listening *to somebody* is more than hearing *something* the Other says. Many linguistic theories forget that there is no mutual understanding and no intention without attention i.e. without something which becomes aroused and which is given or "paid" and not at all produced or exchanged. What we call pathos or affection is marked by features of alienness, of *Ichfremdheit,* before we ascribe it to someone who may have caused it. As we have seen, the gaze or voice are not restricted to the event of becoming visible or audible, they include myself being seen and appealed to. That means that I perceive myself from elsewhere. All this belongs to everyday situations which all have their background of *Unalltäglichkeit* or non-everydayness, but in addition it is deeply anchored in our own genesis. This can be demonstrated by the process of naming. The so-called given name which everybody bears is a half-alien name because it is received from others. I get a *Rufname* by responding to it, whereas an object is not expected to adopt its label. Further, not only my name, but numerous habits and features are incorporated into my social body. Even my own language comes from others so that we call it our mother tongue. In general we must admit that we know our own language from hearsay. Finally, our body is a gendered and sexual body, largely shaped by the desire of the Other. The latter has to be understood in a double way, as the desire I am subject to from the Other and the desire I feel for the Other. Taking into account that the Other is quasi implanted into us from the child's early symbiosis with its mother, we may follow the psychoanalyst Jean Laplanche and admit a certain primacy of the Other. We cannot reach the Other as Other without starting from him or her.

However, that does not mean that we simply reverse the inherited egocentrism and replace it with a sort of allocentrism. It is also true that we cannot start from the Other without referring implicitly to ourselves. But that is not all. In a similar way to how my *Leibkörper* is subject to a continuous scale of nearness and remoteness in relation to myself, my *social body* belongs only more or less to myself, corresponding to a changing degree of nearness and remoteness in relation to others. Intercorporeity implies that the own and the alien are entangled, that everybody is inserted into an interlacing, into a *Geflecht* or *entrelacs* as Norbert Elias, Merleau-Ponty and sometimes even Husserl put it (see above p. 18). There are no ready-made individuals, rather there is only a process of individualisation which presupposes a certain anonymity and typicality of our bodily self. What we feel, perceive, do or say is interwoven with what others feel, perceive, do or say. What one (*man*) does or says does not inevitably sink to the level of *Uneigentlichkeit* or *Vulgarität* (inauthenticity or commonness). Rather it constitutes the anonymous background of what we do or say in our own name. And that is not all, somebody who receives his or her name and does not simply have it keeps a certain zone of namelessness in his or her heart. Ancient prohibitions on using names or making images point to an inviolability of ourselves which cannot be conceived without a certain alienness and remoteness of our body. Consequently we must assume that our body functions as a "transfer-point" (*Umschlagstelle*), not only inasmuch as doing and undergoing, culture and nature are involved but also in respect to the intertwining of the own and the alien. To speak of "my own body" or of a *corps propre* expresses only half of the truth. In his theory of the novel Mikhail Bakhtin develops the perspective of an "inner dialoguicity" of speaking. In this context he claims that each word is a "half-alien word" because it is "charged, even overcharged by others' intentions" (1979, p. 185). In a similar way I suggest that my own body is a half-alien body, charged and even overcharged by intentions, but also desires, projections, habits, affections and violations coming from others.

In the end our bodily experience shows that I find the Other within myself and myself within the Other before we encounter each other. The Other appears within me and at my side before appearing in front of me. And even when facing the Other I do not stand with him or her on the same level. Our intercourse takes place on an inclined plane on which it is always the Other who occupies the upper part, the height as Levinas puts it. This strange, multiplied asymmetry is not due to my attitude — it is not as if it were up to me to prefer the Other's existence to my own interests. Our bodily experience of the Other has nothing to do with the 18th century's altruism in which it constitutes only the corrective counterpart to an egoism which is taken for granted. In the beginning of myself it is not me who prefers the Other or does not, it is rather experience itself which pre-fers. Just as any affect, as long as it is not normalised and channelled, surprises us, the affection by others overcomes us. Summing up our former formulations we can say: birth out of pathos, concerning sense and myself, leads back to a sort of *allopathos,* concerning others. After all, our bodily experience is not comfortable. We will never completely be settled in our own body as if we were the owner of ourselves. But it may be that it is just this disquiet which keeps us alive.

Lecture VI

Violence as Violation

Opening: *Sacrifice of human beings.* — Violence has many faces. One is that of the sacrifice. The following case is taken from the field of ethnopsychiatry.[1] It concerns an Arab living in Germany who was brought to trial because he had killed or, as he put it, sacrificed his own daughter i.e. the most beloved being he had. Obviously he was a psychopath as the expert in forensic medicine certified. But though it may well have been madness yet there was some method or, to put it in better terms, some tradition to it. Who would not be reminded of the sacrifice of Isaac? Except that in this case no heavenly Third Party came to intervene, no saving angel appeared as in Abraham's story, well known from many paintings. Anyone who finds this example all too archaic should take a look at the numerous heroic monuments where we can still read epitaphs of the type: "Wherever heroes are buried is Holy Land. They died so that we may live in peace." Who sacrifices whom for what? Nevertheless, there remains the question as to whether sacrifice rituals, in spite of the ideological misuse that is made of them and in spite of the violence they carry with them, do not retain some features of an excessive giving which is lost if everything has its price.

* * *

Our following reflections are not based on the assumption that violence is something which has its own essence, nor do they presuppose that there are normal acts of violence which have a certain meaning and follow certain rules, as if violence simply belongs to our being in the world. On the contrary, violence seems to be something strange. It resembles phenomena such as love and death, phenomena traversing various domains of life, striking us as something ungraspable, insoluble, extraordinary, questioning all order, something with no proper place. The peculiarity of violence is shown by the fact that in antiquity it appears in a mythical form, as do Kronos, Eros and Thanatos. With no secure place of its own, it gives rise to peculiar aporias. In Hannah Arendt's words, violence confronts us with the task "to think the unthinkable" (1970, p. 6). If violence could be conceived as something which simply belongs to the life of individuals and peoples, it would affect us like a virus. To think violence means to think against it.

Such a difficult issue requires a proceeding which approximates the phenomenon in an indirect way, marking the aporias we are confronted with. Hence I shall begin with a selection of topics which encircle the phenomenon, taking into consideration various points of view and taking a look into the corresponding linguistic field. What seems to be especially important is to see that violence is a cultural phenomenon which cannot be transposed to some kind of brute nature. However the leading idea will consist of the assumption that violence has to do with a violation that befalls somebody. This leads us to further questions concerning the state of the perpetrator and the state of the victim. As to the first we have to ask to what extent the actor can be regarded as responsible, and as to the latter we have to take into account a sort of singularity which exceeds the different paths of normalisation such as legalisation, medicalisation, moralisation or historisation. Our reflections will end by testing different ways of legitimisation which all seem to miss the strange character of violence.

The way we proceed can be characterised as phenomenological in so far as we go beyond categories, regulations, arguments and evaluations of all sorts, raising the question as to how violence appears, how it invades the field of experience and how it is expressed in language. Phenomenology is not as naive as some people pretend. It does not presuppose that what appears is completely outside of language, but it does presuppose that what happens and appears to us is more than what can be said about it and what can be argued for or against it. The crucial point is not to assume that there is something given outside of language, but to concede that language precedes itself. Seeing and saying and even saying and doing will never coincide. These general considerations touch directly on our issue of violence. If philosophers skip the genealogy of violence and, in a broader perspective, the genealogy of morals they simply beg the question, preserving their good moral conscience and leaving the rest to judges, doctors and the military.

Topics of Violence

Violence arises at the intersections of various orders. Thus it transforms our own *body* into a sphere of vulnerability up to the point of violence against life and limb. *Technology* originates as body technique, and from the very beginning it creates not only tools with which we work on things, but also weapons with which we attack beings like ourselves. Tools are in themselves double-edged things. It was an axe with which Cain killed his brother. "I wish David had killed Goliath with a lyre" says the Polish aphorism writer Stanislaw J. Lec.[2] Just as the body functions as the first instrument, it also functions as the first weapon. Our hand clenches into a fist, our elbow moves forward like a club. But nowadays, relying on modern weapons of destruction which are no longer used or operated as instruments or machines but are turned on and off as an apparatus, we have moved a considerable distance from bodily violence. Violence can be so clean that traces of blood have an atavistic or even an obscene effect. Nor are *games* exempt from violence even if we think of the largely ritualised and regulated jousting of the knights at chivalrous tournaments or of boxing matches. *Religion* is just as deeply impregnated with violence in terms of sacrifices which are offered to a higher power. The ritual or ascetic character of human or animal sacrifices, circumcision, mortification and castigation set these apart from the violence of simple fighting. In Freud's view joint patricide is a primal event in which the community of brothers is founded. The ambiguity of *sacrificium* and *victima* belongs to the semantics of "violence" and gives it explosive features. Finally there is our *language*, which not only speaks *about* violence, but also speaks the language *of* violence. The linguistic scale extends from verbal acts such as insult or threat, through bearing witness to violence, up to its legitimisation. It is almost superfluous to mention the official domains of law, morals and politics. Crimes of violence, the state monopoly on the use of force and violence, and the oscillation between using and exploiting the labour force and natural forces all belong to the traditional problematic.

On the conceptual level violence is difficult to demarcate (cf. Röttgers 1990). The German word *Gewalt* is ambiguous. It covers a double meaning including on the one hand *potestas*, the authority vested in public office (*Amtsgewalt*) and controlled by the separation of powers (*Gewaltenteilung*), and on the other hand *violentia*. In its immediate vicinity we find the term "power" (*potentia, dynamis, Macht*), and its environment includes items such as "force" as an effective power which collides with counter-force, "constraint," which is characterised by impediments and coercion, "conflict" as the clash of forces and interests, "repugnance" as the incompatibility of experiences and attitudes, and a sort of "polemics" without which politics would be a mere epiphenomenon. As to the use of language we must say that too narrow a concept would be apt to curtail the horizon of the problem, whereas too broad a concept would tend to water down the problematic.

Furthermore, we shall have to distinguish special modes of seeking access to violence and of dealing with it. The classical distinction between participation and observation falters. On the one hand, should we assume that the victim of violence "takes part" in the act of violence, perhaps by lack of resistance? On the other hand, is there anything like "pure observation"? We know that to do nothing more than to take note of what is going on could be punishable, for example as failure to lend assistance or as condoning a crime. And where are the limits of what can be reasonably required of the third party who is expected to run a risk by intervening? What about the system-theoretical distinction between drawing a distinction and observing it? To what extent is it possible to describe violent acts in terms of merely systematic procedures? These questions suffice to indicate to what extent our everyday and our academic ways of thought can be shaken by violence.

Finally, I would like to raise an objection on my home ground which mutatis mutandis may also be applied to analytical philosophy. Phenomenology and hermeneutics are dominated by the category of *sense* or *meaning*, which originates from processes of intending, understanding and rule-following. And here the question is whether violence has a sense and whether acts of violence have a meaning which could be explicated, interpreted and appropriated. Should we not rather assume that violence appears as something out of place, as a sort of *foreign body* which disturbs and interrupts the economy of sense? This is where a particular dispute among historians will break out. What seems to be at stake is not the divergence of historical perspectives, trends of interpretation and methodological approaches, it is rather History as such (something which did not exist for the ancient Greeks or for far-eastern cultures) that has to be put to the test. The questions arising here do not inevitably lead to a dubious sort of *posthistoire*. They may just as well lead to an alternative historiography which would no longer be prepared to eliminate every sort of rupture and irruption by means of interpretation and explanation. The "stumbling logic," inherent in the course of history (cf. Merleau-Ponty 1988, p. 85), would find its counterpart in a stammering sort of historiography.

Violence between Nature and Culture

There is a certain trend which is difficult to eradicate. I mean the attempt to locate violence in a pre-historical state of nature which we are so lucky to have left behind us. The repeated irruptions of barbarity into civilised regions are reduced to mere forms of relapse. We act as if we could contemplate the waves of violence from a safe haven. Such attempts to stem violence go back to the beginnings of Western cultural history. *Kratos* and *Bia*, force and violence, which in Aeschylus' *Prometheus Bound* appear in a personalised form, yield their power to the imperium of *Techne*. Cicero's *De officiis* presents two ways to overcome conflicts: the human way of dispute (*disceptatio*) and the animal way of blind violence (*vis*). Regarded from the perspective of world history, the well-known path from darkness to light, from brute beginnings to moral sophistication is opened up. But this does not silence dissenting voices which contradict this all too beautiful and simple fable.

Dissenting voices, which since the days of Rousseau increasingly contest thinking in terms of progress, suggest that violence finds its place, or better its non-place, on the *threshold between nature and culture*. As our dreams demonstrate every night and every day, this threshold will never be definitively crossed. As far as our issue is concerned, this means that violence displays certain features which cannot be banished to the beginnings or to the dark corners of our history. Wherever real progress takes place in the course of history, the old saying bears repeating: *corruptio optimi pessima*, corruption of the best is the worst.

Thus we have to consider some basic features of violence. First, there is the *cultural* character of violence, in contrast to a mere brute or natural sort of violence. Wars and revolutions are completely different from the avalanches or volcano eruptions to which they often are compared. In the last century this naturalisation often had a rather vitalistic air, for example when we listen to the fanfares which accompanied the outbreak of World War I.

Further, the violence which human beings do to each other takes on *symbolic* forms. It is mediated by artificial signs, rituals, practices, tactics and interpretations. It may be sufficient to consider the discourse of war which includes things like the law of war, the declaration of war, war enemy, prisoner of war and war crime. Wars are waged, they do not simply occur. Supposedly brute and naked violence always appears well formed, dressed and armed, and so-called brute force (*Brachialgewalt*) is assisted by head and heart. There are no violent basic actions unless one abstracts rather artificially from the semantics and pragmatics of the violent event. As Hobbes stresses, violent acts are *deemed to be* manslaughter, an act of self-defence, an interrogation under torture and so on. Politics, which is permeated by violence, starts with the act of naming prior to acts of decision-making and judging. To take an example from our contemporary history, it makes a great difference whether the events of 1954 in Budapest or those of 1989 on the Place of Heavenly Peace in Peking are classified as a counter-revolution or as a popular revolt. The difference begins with the right to a burial (which is so important in Sophocles' *Antigone*), and it ends with the legal rights of the surviving dependants. Similar remarks could be made about more recent events. The question as to whether the bloody events in Bosnia should be classified as an ethnic conflict or as a genocide had considerable consequences. The first alternative only called for a neutral intervention, whereas the second one required that the process be stopped by all possible means. The fact that Srebenica (the place of violence in Bosnia where thousands of Bosnian men were led away by Serb soldiers to be killed — before the eyes of the UN troops when we had given a guarantee for those who had laid down their weapons) became a kind of turning-point certainly does not imply that things happened previously in a more moral way. The declaration of the French Parliament in June 1998 that "France officially recognises the Armenian genocide of 1915" belongs to a highly delayed politics of language. The fact that only 29 of the 580 deputies were present makes the symbolic value shrink. But linguistic politics also includes extraordinary attempts to lend words to the singular suffering which nonetheless remains unspeakable, it includes attempts to snatch from the jaws of silence events which cannot be simply classified. Thus the genocide committed on the Armenians and Jews has been given names such as *Grand Crime, Grande Souffrance, Catastrophe, Holocaust* or *Schoa.*[3]

Violence and Violation

After this first circumscription of the phenomenon, we have to ask what is at issue in the case of violence. What is at stake when violence occurs? What are we speaking about when we speak of violence? Is there a semantic nucleus which criss-crosses the multiple variations of violence? In what follows I shall pick out a central motif which is suggested in particular by the Latin word *violentia* and its derivations in the Romance languages. Violence will be shown to be a sort of *violation* which under certain circumstances will increase to become paralysing and long-lasting forms of trauma. But at this point we are showered by questions.

1. From the victim's point of view the question arises: *Who* or *what* can be violated? There are three possibilities: something, somebody or a general rule. Let us start with the possibility that something is violated. If we adhere to everyday and even legal usage, we must admit that simple things can be damaged or destroyed, but certainly not violated. Violence presupposes a certain *self-referentiality* and *integrity* which does not exist in the case of simple function bearers. Something which exists for the sake of something else and not for its own sake cannot be injured in its being, it may only be impaired in its function, for example if a chair looses a leg or a tube leaks. When certain functions are impaired we only speak of damage, which may be slight or grave. The German word *Kriegsbeschädigter* tends to blur this distinction in opposition to the English expression *disabled veteran* or the French expression *mutilé de guerre.* If we accept the proposed distinction it seems reasonable to interpret what is called

violence against things as an indirect violence against persons.

Let us go on to the second possibility. A general *rule* is infringed or violated if somebody does what is forbidden or does not do what is prescribed. But this provides no more help in grasping the full meaning of violence. It is true that murder or manslaughter are regarded as legal or moral crimes, but it is not true that every case of breach of a rule, for example failure to observe the proper period of notice when terminating employment or giving false evidence in court, is taken to be an act of violence. Moreover there are legal forms of deprivation of freedom, execution or killing in war. What makes them acts of violence must be something different from a violation of law.

There remains the third possibility, ascribing the violation to somebody *to whom* it is done. Thus, violence has an addressee, someone from whom life is taken, to whom death is given or to whom something is done. This form of dative has been called addressee dative by Karl Bühler (1984, § 15, Engl. ch. 15). This means that verbs like "murder," "insult" or "rape" are used as three-valued predicates: *somebody* does *something to somebody*. This aspect of the dative, which belongs to the deep structure of doing to (*Antun*) just as it belongs to the deep structure of speaking to (*Anrede*), is dissipated when we reduce acts of violence to legal or moral cases. In so doing we judge such acts from the position of a third party, and we take it as something which somebody (in the nominative) has done on his or her own initiative or on behalf of others. However the victim of violence puts a limit to the processes of legalisation and moralisation, which both tend to make the victim of a deed (*Tat*) disappear behind the legal definition of the crime (*Tatbestand*) under which the deed is subsumed. Moreover we should avoid identifying somebody to whom violence is done with a person to whom certain rights and duties are ascribed. There are pre-legal and pre-moral claims which demand to be listened to and to be looked at, which provoke a responsive mode of hearing and seeing. Such claims arise before they are subjected to the binary criteria of right or wrong.[4] The famous slogan "My country, right or wrong," pronounced by myself, should be balanced by the prior saying "My face, right or wrong," heard from the Other. If it is transposed into a general legal or moral claim, the Other's situated claim would be nothing more than a particular case. Finally, we should take into account the possibility that there are not only human but also non-human addressees of violence.

This use of the difference between something and somebody is far from trivial. A wide-spread form of violence is based on the transformation of somebody into something or on the transformation of the addressee into a goal-object. Let me cite some famous examples. In his *Politics* (I, 2) Aristotle defines the slave as an "animated tool" which is only made use of and not spoken to, except in the computer-like language of directive orders. John Locke, an honourable, liberal man, does not hesitate to declare: "One may destroy a man who makes war upon him, or has discovered an enmity to his being, for the same reason that he may kill a wolf or a lion ..." (*Second Treatise of Government*, III, 16). The slave has never been human, the enemy stops being human, in both cases violence is done *to something*. Today the so-called axis of evil is the hotbed for a new sort of monsters, exempt from human or legal rights. By mixing the features of thing and person we generate hybrids which belong to a special grammar of violence.

2. With regard to the course of a criminal act, the question arises: *In what form* has somebody been violated or injured? Here we run into dubious distinctions such as *bodily* violence and *mental* cruelty. *Symbolic* violence, which is implemented by calumny, threat and insult, is distinguished from real violence, which leads to robbery or killing. But such distinctions always tend to play off one form of violence against the other, as if for example an attack on the Other's dignity were less offensive than a punch. Once again the ordering hand intervenes before violence finds its own language. Such faults of prejudgement can be avoided if we start from an integrated sphere of life, namely *bodily existence as a sphere of vulnerability*. The old proverb according to which we learn by suffering refers to the fact that there are experiences, *Widerfahrnisse*, which occur to us or befall us before we take the initiative. These strong experiences, which have already been presented in the preceding lectures, are accompanied by forms of violation which we only become aware of afterwards. The ambiguous character of bodily experience, which is never completely harmless, finds complex expression in the Greek word *pathos*. Our body must not only be resurrected as a "great reason," as in Zarathustra's speech against the "despisers of the body (*Verächter des Leibes*)" (see above p. 66), it must also be understood as the place of

an all-penetrating violence. Because it is visible, tangible and open to attack, even to mortal attacks, our body forms a territory which opens the door to violence. Our body spreads through the world. It has its surroundings, formed by clothes, everyday tools, dwelling, home country, property and relatives. That is the reason why the requirement to wear a uniform or degrading forms of nakedness, burglary and trespass, expulsion, ban of language and collective liability of the members of a family are the home grounds for indirect forms of violence which affect the Other detrimentally by a sort of *Mitleidenschaft* (co-suffering). Blackmail always takes such an indirect path. Instead of dividing the field of violence into a dualistic pattern, we should look for finer distinctions. Thus we could distinguish between a *peripheral* and a *central* form of violence, referring to a scale which extends from the insistent gaze through lewd remarks and offensive conduct to torture, rape and murder. Making the further distinction between *direct* and *indirect* violence enables us to trace the evasive manoeuvres of violence as in the case of reprisals. Similarly to how Freud separates the *Triebziel* (drive goal) from the *Triebobjekt* (drive object), we can distinguish between the more steady goal and the more variable object of violence. Finally, there is a difference between *on-going* and *structural* violence. The fact that this distinction may be used to denigrate institutions as a whole should not lead us to personalise violence excessively. In this context it may be helpful to consider the acting and the habitual side of our body. Violence occurs momentarily when we suffer from disregard, attack or injury. But it can also be deposited in our body. There are numerous examples of this: forced labour, which engraves its traces into the body day by day; military drill, which bends the body into shape and makes it interchangeable; the diffusion of an atmosphere of fear, which represses free utterances; discriminating administrative rules or practices, which infringe on the rights of equality; stigmatisation, which extends to the extreme forms of branding slaves or imposing the yellow star of David on Jewish citizens. Whereas structural violence, when restricted to forced labour, preserves a minimum of community, it turns into pure terror when victims are used as deterrents, and it ends with extermination when all victims are equalised by technically and hygienically constructed killing machines.[5]

3. From the side of the perpetrator we have to pose the question:

Who or *what* is responsible for the violation? Do we have to do with acts of violence or with a simple occurrence of violence? What about the originator of violence? The first answer should be: events become actions or deeds by being ascribed to somebody as his or her action. Everybody can more or less participate in what happens. The eclipse of the great subject also undermines the position occupied by the great holders of power and violence, by all sorts of *Macht-* and *Gewalthaber*. Responsibility appears in dosed forms, and the dose is measured in accordance with the different orders of action, of society and of life, all of which distribute chances and allow for initiatives but in different ways. However if nobody were personally involved in committing violence and if nobody were addressed by it, there would be nothing left other than pure operations to be observed and controlled from the neutral position of a third party. The participation perspective would be simply replaced by the observation perspective. This would be another form of violence. The complete incapacitation, the *Entmündigung* of the perpetrator, would simultaneously incapacitate the victims by taking even the word of complaint out of their mouths.

Collective, Individual, and Anonymous Violence

Questioning the functioning of violence we are confronted with further questions, first with the question of the *collective* aspect of violence. John Ladd, who represents an individualistic approach, defines collective violence as "that kind of violence that is practised by one group on another and that pertains to individuals, as agents or as victims, only by virtue of their (perceived) association with a particular group" (Ladd 1991, p. 19). In opposition to the *private* form of violence, the collective form cannot be explained by personal motives like profit-seeking or vindictiveness; such an attempt would be guilty of an "individualisation fallacy" (ibid., p. 23). Such a broad definition of collective violence allows us to include not only war and genocide, but also criminal assassinations when individually committed, lynch justice with an individual victim, or a ritual duel. Concerning the institution of violence there are sharper qualifications at hand: a *massacre* takes place when perpetrator and victim are in a one-sided relationship to each other, a *war* when several hostile groups fight against each other, a *genocide* is when whole populations are exterminated. However in general it seems to me more appropriate to oppose private to *public* violence, corresponding to the distinction between private and public law. This permits us to avoid confusing the institution of violence with its organisation.[6]

Further we must ask how the actions of those who are actively or passively involved in the event of violence are organised and to what extent they can be found guilty in the moral or in the legal sense. In this context we are faced with the alternative of an individualism which reduces the whole event to individual actions or a holism which introduces wholes like people, mass or class as collective agencies. Even if this distinction has to be understood only as a methodological option, the prestige of a corresponding social ontology persists. This ontology is severely shaken by a genealogical approach which takes both, individuals and societies, to be the result of a simultaneous process of individualisation and socialisation, and which presumes that such a process can happen in different ways and to different degrees. A medieval craftsman or a family-bound Chinese person does not show the same individual features as a modern bourgeois or a hypermodern single. Pascal's ascription of all disaster to the fact that we are unable to remain quietly in our own room presupposes a high degree of independence and self-sufficiency. When Foucault raises the question of the author he does not ask "Is there an author?," but rather "What is an author?" Merleau-Ponty's assumption that there is a sort of corporeal-social anonymity at the heart of our being and that this passivity constitutes an "inner weakness which prevents us from ever achieving the density of an absolute individual" (1945, p. 489, Engl. p. 428) also undermines the alternative of individualism or holism. Finally, this view is complemented by the inner polyphony of speech we encounter in Mikhail Bakhtin's literature studies.

Let us now ask about the consequences which all this has with respect to the authorship of violence and the alternative of individual or collective guilt. If we accept the anti-Cartesian and anti-Humean presupposition that there is an intertwining of own and alien, that is, that there is an *Ineinander* (intermingling or intertwining) of speech and counter-speech, of action and counter-action, based on an original form of intercorporeity (see above p. 18), then the single person finds his place within a social field which is not only, but also, a field of violence. This entanglement does not only connect victims and co-victims, perpetrators and accomplices, it even includes the relationship between victim and perpetrator. Jorge Semprun, who certainly is far from glossing things over or covering up injustice, shows very clearly how infamous it is when victims are transformed into accomplices, not only in order to save their own lives, but also in order to prevent things from becoming worse.[7] This is not to blur all distinctions, leading us into the night when all cats are black, in which every kind of responsibility would be extinguished. Rather, it creates a *clair-obscur*, a manifold spectrum of variegated perpetration and complicity, occupying one and the same social field in which forces are unequally distributed up to the point of polarisation into power (*Macht*) and powerlessness (*Ohnmacht*).[8] Moralists who want to make the situation of violence less ambiguous than it is by strictly separating light and shadow, good and evil, do not only falsify what is going on, they also harm the victims. They demand from them an excess of morality, selflessness or heroism — as if not even victims had a right to normality. Victims are not victims because they are saints or heroes. The fact that there are extraordinary men and women who have taken a greater risk and have given more of themselves than others awakes and merits our admiration. But even the "ordinary" victim deserves our respect.[9]

The anonymity of violence is based on the embodiment of our body which will never be completely our own body, but has something of a *Fremdkörper, a foreign body*, something of a body out of place. This genuine anonymity is reinforced by an excess of technification which increasingly transforms violent acts into mechanisms and operations of violence. The history of war is full of striking examples. Pressing a button or remote controlling a movement are far removed from the thrust of the bayonet or from the gun smoke of the trenches. Decisions calculated by computer require computer-like implementations. Actions resemble distant stars which are already extinguished when we see them. It may be that technological processes need tele-morals which take into account instant long-distance effects and "*Fernstenopfer*" or distant victims, and not only later effects. But such morals would be rather schematic and would vanish in technological networks if we fail to become at the same time "good neighbours of the nearest things."

Normality and Singularity of Violence

The anonymisation of violence is accompanied by another problematic which could be called the normalisation of violence. I shall not unfold this problematic in its full length, but I want to exhibit what has an immediate effect on violation by violence. I begin with a methodological alternative which plays an important role in the human and social sciences with regard to the question of collective violence. An anonymity of violence which cannot be reduced to individual intentions and interests calls for a *structural* method. In accordance with this method, individual positions, actions and ideas are treated as variables which even allow for statistical registration and which are far removed from the *Haupt- and Staatsaktionen,* the pomp and circumstance about which Marx makes ironic comments. With such preconditions, it is not impossible to speak of a normal concentration camp guard and vice versa of a normal concentration camp prisoner, although they have a horrible and frightening normality (H. Arendt 1995, p. 326) and although the "banality of evil" is far from being banal itself. However the structuralist treatment does not preclude the complementary possibility of taking account of individual modes of experience which can be explored by means of oral history, using biographical evidence and, assuming it is not too late, narrative interviews. Both approaches, the structure-orientated and the experience-bound, have their own merits and there is no reason to play off subjects against structures.[10]

The problem seems to arise elsewhere. A structural-functionalist or systemic approach would have to treat even victims as typical or as statistical cases. Consequently the suffering of victims would pertain to the functional equivalencies which sustain or threaten a system. There is nothing against this, just as there is no reason not to draw up lists of crime rates or accident statistics. Anomalous states, which due to their character as crime or illness deviate from normal feeling or behaviour, can be normalised. We do so whenever we speak of a normal *Gestapo* officer, a normal *Stasi* collaborator, or a normal heart attack. Further, in the face of such generalisations it is not sufficient to insist on *individual* victims, suffering and violations. The individual as something of which something is predicated without being itself a possible predicate (the Aristotelian definition) appears as a *Dies-da,* a this-here (τόδε τι); but that already sheds the light of general determinations on it. In terms of modern thinking, the individual forms the intersection of different rules, or it presents itself as a deviation within a social field. The individual is something or somebody else, that is all; it will never be totally other because in this case it would fall out of the frame of determination. The debates about the victims of the Nazis take a completely wrong track when on the one hand they remain on the level of general conceptualisation and on the other hand insist on the uniqueness and incomparability of Auschwitz. A concentration camp can of course be compared to Gulags or to the Inquisition and the persecution of witches as long as violence is considered as something which finds its place (where else?) in some region of the world and in the field of history.

If we claim that suffering is unspeakable this must not be understood in the sense of the old dictum: *individuum est ineffabile.* This sentence means only that nothing which appears here and now is exhausted by general determinations. The old statement: "The concept of dog does not bark" finds its equivalent in a corresponding statement: "The concept of victim does not suffer." If we consider the victim of violence there is much more at stake, namely the fact that the other's claim is violated and not only a general law infringed. First of all the act of violence is *not a topic about which* we talk with others, but an action, directed at an *addressee to whom* it is done. This action lives on in one's own witness and in that of others. Bearing witness does not only mean speaking *about* an event, but rather *from* an event, making it known. The witness does not give a direct account of what is the case, rather it pronounces the way in which something comes into view and is expressed, and this is something that can only be shown and said *afterwards.* This is the origin of the belatedness of traumatic experiences which since Freud has received such strong emphasis,[11] and the same holds for the entanglement of forgetting and remembering in which the horrible events persist. Traumatic events which are impregnated with violence are not marked merely by individuality, but by a sort of *singularity* which goes beyond every ordinary order of action and life. This uniqueness is not only expressed in an excess of suffering, but in outbursts of hatred. These have to be regarded as irrational not only because they run out of control (they can indeed be stimulated and provoked, as we all know), they are ir-rational because they surpass all measure and generate an affective surplus which is acted out in acts of annihilation. The extraordinary that makes itself felt here is not located in a celestial or infernal after-world, it is something strange within this world. Just like other forms of the extraordinary it takes place by disturbing and interrupting the various orders of our world. We call something singular that in the process of "comparing the incomparable" (Levinas 1974, p. 202) proves to be incomparable; and this does not mean that the victim's suffering is completely other or different, but that it is "other than Being," far removed from the reign of ordinary speaking and calculating. It will never find *its place* in the world and it will not find *its place* in history which — despite Hegel's averment — is not able to heal all wounds without leaving scars.[12] It is in this sense that Auschwitz, a name standing for innumerable other places of violence, is incomparable, beyond every comparison, a black hole in the web of history. Singularity occurs in the plural (see above p. 29). One does no injustice to the victims of the Nazis by also conceding singularity to the victims of the Gulags or to the victims of the Armenian or Bosnian genocide. On the contrary, those who elevate Auschwitz to the highest evil, to the *summum malum* of history, themselves make use of a comparative scale.[13]

Violence under the Sway of Order

Assuming that violence is culturally and historically variable according to the orders in which it appears and assuming that this is what gives it its collective shape, then the genealogy of violence forms a junction with the genealogy of orders. This association of order and violence will be our last issue. It is only in this context that violence takes on a clear shape and its historical colouring. We can distinguish different strategies of rationalisation.

Violence against order, violence against reason and right means that one opposes to non-reasonable violence a non-violent reason. Consequently violence seems to be pure *disorder* and lack of reason. This antithesis is too beautiful to be true. Reason and violence encounter each other within this world. They intermingle. They cannot be assigned to an upper world of light and an underworld of darkness.

Violence in the service of order makes it possible to sanctify and rationalise violence to some extent. One relies on a *felix violentia* which, similar to the *felix culpa*, is on the path towards a non-violent order and derives its justification from this fact. The integration of violence into a process which surpasses it leads to the well-known distinctions between just and unjust war, revolution and counter-revolution, or progressive and regressive violence. These distinctions are themselves sources of violence because they lower the threshold of violence. In Western history in particular, violence tends to be ideologically charged and veiled. There is no appeal against *legitimated* violence. The trend to justify violence increases in the 19th century because the demarcation line between legitimate and illegitimate is increasingly transposed into the immanence of history, with the effect that there is no longer a backdoor for reprieve and forgiveness. Things prove to be more modest in the liberal tradition where, since the time of John Locke, violence is taken as the *ultima ratio*,[14] as *emergency violence* or as *counter-violence*. Whereas the former remains in contact with *Notwehr*, self-defence, the latter starts up a machinery of legitimisation which will not come to a stop because in each case the other's violence is declared to be violence, whereas one's own violence is counter-violence.[15] Things become even more modest when this material debate is replaced with formal procedures whose correctness is the only criterion in questions of legitimacy and illegitimacy of violence. What remains could be called *procedural* violence. Violence manifests itself as a source of friction or noise within the machinery of functioning orders which are fighting for their own existence.

The over-rationalisation of violence, which tries to justify or legitimate what is unjustifiable, will never cease to provoke reprisals in terms of *violence in revolt against every order*. The over-rationalisation corresponds to a militant irrationality which explicitly adopts an anarchic form of violence. Oscillating between a utopia of non-governance and the pure destruction of structures of dominion, this kind of violence leads into a dead end.

Violence in the Shadow of Orders

Is there any way out of this vicious circle of power on the endless path of self-intensification and self-preservation? It would be a considerable help to take the *contingency of all order whatsoever* seriously. If all order can be different than it actually is, no order will ever be completely legitimised. The inevitable selectivity and exclusivity, inherent to the character of every order that it is "thus and not otherwise," implies a certain measure of force. Just as we say of an interpretation that it "does violence" to what is interpreted, or as we speak of trenchant measures, we must assume that there is something violent about order. There is no speech, no action, no gaze, no communication which does complete justice to the claims of those who are involved. There will always remain something which is alien (*fremd*), extra-ordinary because it does not find its place within the given order. *Fremdheit* (otherness and alienness) and violence are very close to each other as is suggested by the meaning of *hostis*, which oscillates between *hospitality* and *hostility*. Just as we should assume with Merleau-Ponty that "there is" (*il y a*) rationality and sense or with Foucault that "there is" order, but that reason *as such*, sense *as such*, order *as such* do not exist in the sense of a *singulare tantum*, we should admit that *there is something* violent which is the reverse of order. The adjective form "violent" (*gewaltsam*) may suggest that violence takes place in a parasitic form and not in the substantive form of "violence" (*Gewalt*), not as a substance of violence which would lead us back onto the tracks of Gnosis.[16]

Apart from the violent aspect which results from the contingency of order, violence is to be found in every form of apparent legitimisation and exaggerated sense-giving that we have mentioned. Every attempt to derive the fact that there is violence, a fact that depends on prior forms of primal oblivion and primal perversion, from some other source leads into the maelstrom of a sort of self-made violence — unless one is content with mythical narrations which only *present* what cannot be *explained*. Besides, there is no reason why practical philosophy should be more anxious to provide explanations than is theoretical physics, which after all has it that the cosmos started with a big bang. To show that the inexplicable is inexplicable does not mean that we veil something we do not want to take notice of; on the contrary, mystification starts with the explanation of the unexplainable. Historians may dismiss these reflections as futile speculations far removed from reality, but they would be wrong. As history shows, exaggerated visions which admit of realisation tend to be exceptionally effective.

If there is something like a fact of violence, then it is not up to us to choose it; there are only various ways of treating it. Even renouncing violence takes place *in and by* speaking and doing, that is, within a field which is already marked by violence. The attempt to think the unthinkable finds its practical resonance in the attempt to do the impossible — im-possible insofar as it surpasses the range of given possibilities and existing rules, and in the attempt to do it again and again and not once for all. Let me finish with a text passage, taken from Jorge Semprun's novel *What a Beautiful Sunday!* The Spanish author, himself a burnt child who dreads the fire, burnt not only by violence but also by ideologies of violence, quotes Merleau-Ponty and Malraux: "There are just wars, but no just armies," and himself continues: "There are just wars, but no innocent armies." However we select and distribute the adjectives one thing seems to be sure: any (definitive) solution of the question of violence would itself be a violent solution.

Lecture VII

Being Here and Elsewhere

Opening: *Contract of conquest.* — Questions of space and place have a political aspect in so far as there is no common life without territories and frontiers. Our last opening scene reminds us of the history of colonisation. It refers to the taking possession of new lands as a basic and official form of appropriation. An instruction issued by the Spanish king in 1514 describes in all details the formal acts which have to be observed:

> The manner you must have in the taking of possession of the lands and parts which you will have discovered is to be that, being in the land or part that you shall have discovered, you shall make before a notary public and the greatest possible number of witnesses, and the best known ones, an act of possession in our name, cutting trees and boughs, and digging or making, if there be an opportunity, some small building, which should be in a part where there is some market hill or a large tree, and you shall say how many leagues it is from the sea, a little more or less, and in which part, and what signs it has, and you shall make a gallows there, and have somebody bring a complaint before you, and as our captain and judge you shall pronounce upon and determine it, so that, in all, you shall take the said possession; which is to be for that part where you shall take it, and for all its district and province or island, and you shall bring testimony thereof signed by the said notary in manner to make faith.[1]

This sophisticated procedure finds its legal basis in Roman law, according to which taking possession (*occupatio*) is legitimate as far as there is no former owner who contradicts and registers a complaint. But in what language and in what form should the so-called natives have complained? The complaint as set forth in the instruction already presupposes a legitimate rule which prescribes how to take possession, and this rule goes back to the whole tradition of Spanish-Roman law. The rules of the game and of language are imposed, and what may well belong to the Other has already been institutionally appropriated by the conquerors before the proceedings are opened. What is to be thought of Columbus's statement in his diary that nobody had contradicted him? Is this an expression of black humour or of cynicism? And further, can we really say that questions as to who takes possession of land and in what way it is done have lost their importance in the era of global networks, or are they only complemented by other forms of space occupation?

* * *

Our last lecture will approach the phenomenon of otherness or alienness from the perspective of human embodiment in place or space. Accordingly, the topological aspect of alienness, which has been emphasised from the very beginning of our *tour d'horizon*, will enter into a larger context. Our reflections will proceed in two steps and on two levels. On the first level the well-known phenomenology of body and space will be presented against the background of Western cosmology and anthropology. By mean of this rough sketch these achievements will be given a certain historical depth. This can help us to assess properly what phenomenology has to offer in this area. Even if it is true that phenomenological descriptions differ considerably from historical investigations dealing with multiple and cross-cultural interpretations of body, space and senses, they have their own right. In addition, they could prevent historical and cultural studies from disintegrating and from reducing the excess and the appeal of the alien to mere variations of what has been the case. On the second level of our considerations the phenomenological conceptions of body and space will be problematized in a new way. By driving these conceptions to certain paradoxes we will raise a series of questions which all revolve around a certain not-place of the alien. Our lectures will finish with some current issues concerning the process of so-called globalisation.

Three Historical Space Paradigms

In the course of history we can distinguish three great paradigms of space centred on the key concepts of *topos*, *spatium* and *Lebenswelt*. The variety of the corresponding terms and the changes they have undergone are highly significant; this aspect excludes a simple continuity of one and the same topic and points to deep historical changes concerning our world orientation and even our dwelling in the world. Phenomenology seems to be able to cope with this multiplicity only by transforming Husserl's eidetic phenomenology, which relies on invariant basic structures, into a structural phenomenology that reckons with variable structures.[2] In addition to this, it is to be expected that the multiplicity resulting from historical diachronicity finds a resonance in another multiplicity pertaining to intercultural synchronicity. To some extent, the otherness of our own past and the otherness of other cultures elucidate and reinforce each other. Whereas ethnology can be defined as research of what is culturally alien, historiography deals in part with what is temporally alien. This sort of alienness, penetrating investigations which, as scientific projects, methodologically abstract from particular views and interests, goes back to certain places in the world and in history from which, and only from which, alienness appears as alienness. In so far as alienness pertains to the things themselves, phenomenology for its part, when trying to describe the phenomenon of alienness, takes on certain features of what may be called xenology (see Lecture I).

Let us begin with the concept of *topos*. Understood in terms of Aristotelian physics, *topos* means that within the cosmos everything (and everybody) has its own or proper place, its *oikeios*[3] or *idios topos*, just as it has its proper time, its *kairos*. All particular places are integrated into the *koinos topos*, the common place, constituted by the order of the universe, by the *Weltall*. This totality encompasses all that exists. Things envelop each other in such a way that they are inside and outside each other like Russian dolls. Thus the room is part of the house, the house part of the neighbourhood, the neighbourhood part of the city, the city part of the country and so on. Only the universe as a whole is something which nothing is outside of (οὗ μηδὲν ἔξω: Aristotle, *Physics* III, 6, 207 a 8). The limits of the *cosmos* as a whole coincide with the limits constituted by a unique *topos*. Even human beings belong to this all-embracing order whose members are all characterised by self-movement (*hautokinesis*) and goal-orientation (*entelecheia*). Thus not only living or human beings strive for certain goals, the physical elements do so too: heavy bodies tend to the centre of the earth, fire rises towards heaven, both tending in this way to their natural place in the universe. Plato's conception of the world-body and the world-soul, for the most part unfolded in his important dialogue *Timaeus*, does not have a merely archaic, animistic sense; rather, it results from defining life by self-movement, so that the cosmos emerges as a great living being.

The *topos* survived to the medieval period, although reinterpreted in connection with the order of creation, but in the modern era with the development of physics in the Cartesian interpretation it changes into *spatium*, a skeleton-like space which has lost its cosmic flesh. This new space looks like a container, reduced to a void scheme which is occasionally filled by something or other. All qualities that once belonged to the cosmic *topos* are now radically quantified in terms of *extension*, ascribed to each thing, and in terms of *distance*, separating one thing from another. Things, including human beings, no longer pertain to the environment they inhabit with their own space. On the contrary, everything occurs *anywhere*, located in a homogeneous and isotropic space which is constituted by points, lines and dimensions. Deprived of any finality, the movements of bodies mean nothing other than the change of spatial positions, whereas for Aristotle locomotion (*phora*) was only one form of movement (*kinesis*) among others. This has the consequence that the new space becomes, properly speaking, uninhabitable.

In our time there have been many attempts to return to what Husserl calls the *Lebenswelt*. Life-world means a world inhabited by human beings, all of them bodily dwelling and moving in the world. This far-reaching phenomenological renewal of the ancient world conception has certain affinities not only with what American pragmatists and Wittgenstein have in mind when they refer to the pragmatics of social or socialised actions. It even finds a certain resonance in post-classical physics, beginning with Maxwell's field-theory. Electromagnetic fields have configurations and structures which cannot be explained by the mere interplay of forces and counter-forces. This new orientation is notably supported by ecological tendencies which re-evoke the old concept of *oikos*, though the modern house seems to be deprived of an ever-lasting house order.

At this point another methodological remark should be made.

History does not proceed on a linear path. The above-mentioned paradigms have to be read not only diachronically but also synchronically. Consequently we are faced with a set of interferences, superpositions, anticipations and revivals. New orders, established by deviation from existing orders, never completely absorb or preserve that from which they deviate. Because of their asymmetrical structure, deviations resist all kinds of "superelevation" or *Aufhebung* in the sense of Hegel's dialectic. Where deviation happens there is not something new opposed to something old in terms of thesis and antithesis, but rather the new only exists by deviating from the old. The owl of Minerva takes wing too late to grasp this process *in flagranti.* Let me only mention the superposition of Jewish, Greek and Arabian ideas and practices in Western Culture, or the entanglement of Confucian, Taoist and Buddhist elements within the development of Chinese culture. Finally, with regard to our special topic we can discern a certain tension between the Platonic *chora* and the Aristotelian *topos*, and this tension considerably increased in the time of Galileo when the mathematical constructs of nature led to a rediscovery of Plato's cosmology.

The Multiplicity of the Life-world

Before going into the details of spatial descriptions, something general should be said about the multiple character of what Husserl introduced under the title of life-world. First, Husserl did not by any means long for some lost immediacy of simple life, but rather tried to respond to a genuine, on-going Crisis i.e. to the Crisis of the European Sciences which in his view involved a crisis of life.[4] The radicality of Husserl's concept depends on the fact that in his view the life-world does not really exist as a totality of beings (*omnitudo realitatis*), and that it must also not be conceived as a regulative idea in the Kantian sense. The life-world is certainly given, it is given to me and to us, but in such a way that it is only co-given with whatever appears. The life-world itself has a double function, as the *universal horizon* within which everything appears, and as the *universal ground* from which everything arises. As a universal *towards-which* (*Woraufhin*) and a universal *whence* (*Woher*) it penetrates every intentional sense. So I cannot speak of things within the world without speaking at once of myself and of others living with me in the world. What Merleau-

Ponty calls indirect ontology is precisely what is required by this indirect kind of appearance. If everything which is the case is based in the life-world, the life-world itself is not simply the case. In a certain sense we can say that world happens as worlding (*es weltet*), and this in terms of a *uniqueness* for which the plural makes no sense (Hua VI, 146, Engl. 143). Possible worlds point back to the actual world. The actual world is not merely a world among others, as conceived by the eternal thinking of Leibniz' divine mind; it is rather presupposed by all variations our world may undergo. This "absolute fact" can neither be denied nor can it be deduced from elsewhere. It corresponds to a kind of world belief (*Weltglaube*). Linguistically this belief could be conceived as a set of indispensable presuppositions, which include the reference to the factual world, the auto-reference to myself addressing others and the co-reference to the others I address and I am addressed by. Before affirming or denying anything, we presuppose that there is a world (*es gibt Welt*), and this "there is" goes beyond universality and particularity, beyond ideality and facticity. If we continue calling this fundamental event transcendental, as Husserl surely does, this has nothing to do with mere conditions of possibility which precede experience but rather with an actual form of making possible (*Ermöglichung*). If we take into account that the play and latitude (*Spielraum*) of our possibilities are always restricted because of factual conditions such as our corporeality and our spatial and temporal situation here and now, we must concede that this making possible means at the same time making impossible. Thus the order of the world is to some extent contingent. But to what extent? Do we simply meet with contingency within order, or is contingency inherent in order itself?

At this point some important distinctions have to be made. First we must mention the dimensions of the *concrete* and the *abstract*. With this in mind Husserl distinguishes between a plurality of concrete life-worlds and the universal structures of the one life-world to be "distilled by abstraction" (Hua VI, 136, Engl. 133). Second, we are confronted with the dimensions of the *whole* and the *part* due to the fact that each cultural life-world is divided into a set of particular or professional worlds (*Sonderwelten, Berufswelten*). Third, in addition to this intracultural articulation of the life-world we have to take intercultural worlds into consideration, worlds that vary historically and geographically, and leading e.g. to the world of Chinese peasants that Husserl takes as an example (Hua VI, 141, Engl. 139). However nobody approaches different cultures from some random standpoint or other, rather everybody starts from his or her own culture. So we enter a third dimension i.e. that of one's *own* and the *alien*. Using Husserl's own terms we can say: the life-world is divided into the home-world (*Heimwelt*) and the alien world (*Fremdwelt*). This third dimension in which the own is detached from the alien has been especially important for us and will continue to be so.

Orientated versus Homogeneous Space

Let us now turn to the special question of how the life-world is spatially or topologically organised. Considering the fact that the rehabilitation of the life-world is invoked to overcome naturalistic trends, phenomenological descriptions of space experience usually start from a fundamental distinction i.e. from the distinction between a purely homogeneous space and an orientated type of space without which the own and the alien would be completely out of place.

Within *homogeneous* space we occupy only internal *positions* (or *sites*), and they are all relative, equivalent; something or somebody is *anywhere* or *somewhere or other* (in French: *n'importe où* i.e. it does not matter where). Space schemes consist of points and lines. The void left by these schemes can be filled by anything. Nothing really "takes place." By contrast, things look rather different when we enter *orientated* space. This type of space originally received its name from its relation to the orient, the region of the sunrise, but generally speaking it is orientated on a certain "here" (and "now").[5] This "here" may be the sun's changing position, corresponding to the habits of certain ethnic groups that prefer a strictly heliocentric orientation.[6] In general, the particular "here" becomes privileged among other places because it functions as a *Nullpunkt*, as the zero point from which the various dimensions originate. In the second volume of the *Ideas* (Hua IV, 158) Husserl uses this term, which he adopted from the physiologist E. Hering, and it is not very difficult to grasp its sense. The "here" is neither situated on the right nor on the left, neither above nor below etc. In his *Theory of Language* (1982, pp. 102–107, Engl. pp. 117–122) Karl Bühler treats the "here" linguistically as the *origo* i.e. as the origin of a deictic field (*Zeigfeld*).

As is well known, the adverb "here" belongs to the class of occasional or indexical expressions which are used to indicate the circumstances of the speech, and it points to the place the actual speaker or actor occupies. Here we come across a suture between space experience and speaking, which — by the way — is neglected by many philosophers of language. Indeed, I have to be bodily involved in the situation in order to understand what the indexical expression actually means.[7] "Here" plays a special role by marking a situation from which a world opens, and not only for me, but also for you and for others. Now the orientation which creates such an open space is highly complex, displaying various aspects.

Space dimensions

First we have to distinguish different dimensions. The dimension of *above and below* is connected with the upright position of humans which take the earth as their ground. As Berkeley clearly remarks in his treatise *Towards a New Theory of Vision* (Sect. 101 f.), we do not see simply by means of optical impressions whether something is above or below and whether someone is standing upright or upside down, without using the sense of touch which makes us touch the earth with our feet. Vertical orientation reappears in the "statics" of buildings, which literally means the art of making something stand. Statics requires special skill when the buildings are constructed on rocky slopes as in the higher districts of Hong Kong Island. The rich symbolism surrounding heaven and earth entails an overdetermination of our bodily position which not only occupies a place, but also marks it. The famous free fall studied by Galileo still alludes to this body-dependent dimension, although strictly speaking pure physical bodies, traversing void space in a certain direction and with a certain speed, do not fall at all. They move where they move without being affected by any up or down.

The polarity of *before and behind* derives from the human face as the seat of mouth and eyes, in opposition to the back of our body which is more exposed than posed. Accordingly houses, too, have their facade and their rear, and even the field of perception is organised by being divided into foreground and background.

Finally, we distinguish between *right and left* i.e. between our right and left hand, or nowadays between the right and the left part of the brain. Right and left, pertaining to someone's functioning brain, cannot be *seen* as such as long as the functioning brain is merely *observed as something* by an apparatus like the PET. This third kind of polarity, the opposition between right and left, shows a greater degree of exchangeability than the two others. But it is all the more full of symbolism, even moral and political symbols, the right side turning to rightness, the left side to the sinister — or vice versa, according to different cultural patterns. However, how can we decide where is right and where left? Kant raises this question in his essay *What Does it Mean to Orient Oneself in Thinking?* In his view, orientating oneself means to find out the (sun)rise (*Aufgang*) from a given world region (*aus einer gegebenen Weltgegend*). The solution he proposes looks rather phenomenological: I discover the distinction between right and left by "feeling a distinction in my own subject," located mainly in my own hands (ed. Weischedel, vol. III, p. 308). This elementary example of corporeal thinking precedes other forms of topology, which can be qualified as geographical, as mathematical, as logical or simply as literate, as in the process of writing from left to right or vice versa, or from above to below. When Heidegger and Merleau-Ponty evoke certain dimensions of Being they do more than simply make use of secondary space metaphors, as if the process of thinking itself were completely out of place.

Nearness and distance

This highly dynamic distinction would be completely misunderstood if it were taken as the distance (*Abstand*) from one thing to the other or as a mere interval (*Zwischenraum*) separating things existing in a pre-given space, each placed beside the other in a sort of juxtaposition. Being close by or far away presupposes somebody traversing the space whose movements show a certain range (*Spielraum*) and whose tempi and rhythms differ in accordance with techniques of locomotion. Following Paul Virilio's dromology (1996, p. 74 f., 104), we may distinguish between immediate proximity, simply bound to the moving body; mechanical proximity, dependant on certain means of transport; and electronic proximity, reaching the speed of light. The last step seems to announce an overwhelming tele-presence whose global neighbourhood would be able to create a technological version of omnipresence. We shall come back to this problem.

Inside and outside

The difference between inside and outside looks more simple than it is. There is no inside and outside at all without somebody being *included* by the boundaries of a certain place and being at once *excluded* from other places. Only living beings, qualified as inhabitants of the world, have access to inside and outside. The difference between inside and outside simply vanishes when the world is seen from the bird's-eye view, turning inclusions and exclusions into mere juxtapositions. The difference also disappears when observed from the point of view of a whole, such as the above-mentioned cosmos which has no outside. The contrast between inside and outside is owing to one's own body. Our body is simultaneously separated from and mediated with its physical and social environment by means of its skin. With regard to this elementary constitution of borderlines, the French psychoanalyst Didier Anzieu (1985) speaks of a "skin-ego" (*moi-peau*), and according to Nietzsche even things have their specific skin and surface (*Gay Science*, aph. 256, KSA, vol. 3, p. 517), provided that we consider them as voluminous "things themselves," coexisting with us in the world, not yet reduced to purely flat things (*Flächendinge*).

As was already shown in our first lecture, the contrast between inside and outside becomes crucial as soon as the segregation of what is one's own and what belongs to others (*Eigenes – Fremdes*) is at stake. External limits or frontiers do not exist without somebody transgressing them, at once on this side and on the other side. There are good reasons to assume that the classical thinking of the Greeks was really unable to form a radical concept of *Fremdheit*, of alienness, because the cosmos comprehends everything in such a way that everybody can feel at home in the world. Only the chaotic seems to remain outside the well-ordered universe. And things are only reversed when Gnostics regard the universe as a bad world. In their opinion we all are strangers in the world, living in a great prison. So it looks as if we have only the alternative to live either inside the world or outside, but never both at once.

Spatial dispositions

Space is articulated by the disposition and composition of things and persons, all together forming a common room or a common place. Thus in his work *On Duties* (*De officiis*, I, 40) Cicero defines order as the "composition of things at apt and appropriate places (*compositio rerum aptis et accomodatis locis*)." To some extent order itself can be defined as a spatial order. The articulation of places and rooms oscillates between fullness and emptiness, between parsimony and abundance. Both aspects have to be understood qualitatively: rooms are too full or too empty. Places appear as overcrowded like the infernal scenes of Bosch's paintings, or as empty scenarios like the vedutas of Chirico's *pittura metafisica*. We could also mention the medieval dispute between the abbot Suger of St. Denis, praising the beauty of light and colour, and Bernard of Clairvaux, propagating austerity and severity, in the 12th century; or more recently the attack on the proliferation of historicism by functionalist architects such as Adolf Loos, who regarded ornamentation as a crime. All these fine distinctions make no sense in the void space of classical physics. In opposition to this rigid scheme, flexible orders, originating from lived space, pass through numerous variations, dependent e.g. on the distribution of people's locations in a teaching room, a factory or a restaurant. The whole arrangement may be centred or not, preferring either tables with a head or round tables. Or take the multiplicity of town plans. There are traditional European towns, surrounding a public place (*agora, forum, market* etc.), centred on the town church or the town-hall and, in contrast, non-centred towns like Kyoto which is divided into many temple districts, or American town-landscapes which are spread out like a carpet, or a harbour town like Hong Kong Island, initially occupying a small strip of land, squeezed between rocky hills and the coast, and finally growing to become a gigantic assembly of skyscrapers.

Let me close this section with some additional remarks. First, all the different aspects of lived space are clearly reflected in our every-day-language, not only by adverbs like "here" and "there," but also by space propositions such as "in," "on," "before" and "behind," or "over" and "under." In his *Poetics of Space* (1957, p. 178) Gaston Bachelard postulates a "phenomenology of ex-" to analyse this prefix, which is not as simple as it looks.[8] Second, as Husserl already shows (see especially *Ideas II*), homogeneous space is far from being simply given, it is derived from orientated space by means of homogenisation. Treating "here" *as* a position among others leads to a reciprocity of perspectives and ultimately to a levelling of all perspectives. This process again illustrates what we, with Nietzsche, have defined as a process of "equalising what is not equal" (see above p. 15) — a process which characterises the contingency of order in general. Third, well-established space orders are shaken when normal relations are reversed and the ordinary world turns into a *verkehrte Welt,* when things are topsy-turvy, *drunter und drüber, sens dessus dessous.* Questioning traditional hierarchies, as Mikhail Bakhtin shows in his book on literature and carnival festivals, such reversals suggest that things could be other than they are. This leads us to the second level of our reflections where we will problematise step by step what our descriptions have brought to light.

Real or Symbolic Space?

Is there real space, prior to symbolic representations? Is it true that symbolic space only plays a secondary role? In an attempt to answer these questions, we discover that everybody who relies on the simple distinction between "real" and "symbolic" would be committing a *petitio principii* and reproducing well-known metaphysical prejudices. One simply assumes that there are things inside and things outside space, and one concludes that attributes of the former are metaphorically transferred to the latter. So we would create, as it were, conceptual hybrids like "*high* person," "*right* reason," "logical *exclusion*" or "*inner* world." But we should better ask if there is any something or somebody not previously affected by "place identity" i.e. without *its* place and *its* time, at least to some extent. Is it possible to place Who- and What-questions on the one side and Where-questions on the other? Nietzsche was certainly right to claim that simple What-is-questions (τί ἐστιν) are full of metaphysical implications when taken as fundamental (see also above p. 30, n. 9).

These general assumptions need further explanation. First, the "here" of the speaker and the "there" of the listener do not simply belong to what is *said,* they belong to the very process of *saying* by which speaking literally *takes place* (*findet statt, a lieu*). There always remains something as the place of speaking which cannot be reduced to the propositional content of the speech act, or to the *énoncé* realised by a certain *énonciation.* Such a reduction would ultimately abolish the speech event or the discourse practice, without which nothing would be said. Classical rhetorics had good reasons to take public speech scenes such as the political assembly, the court and the festival arena into consideration. Further, as Erwin Straus clearly shows in his Book *Vom Sinn der Sinne* (1956, Engl. *The Primary World of Senses,* 1963), each sense is intrinsically determined by specific forms of spatiality. Items like localisation, direction or distance do not mean the same when we shift from one sense to the other. Sounds do not simply arise from the place where sound sources are located. We do not encounter sounds as something in front of us; rather, they surround and envelop us. We do not hear one and the same melody in the same way as we see the same tree, because repetition plays a different role in each case. Sounds happen, they are not deeply rooted as trees are. The space of smell must be specified in a similar way, including the smoke of incense candles which passes through the temple hall, creating a particular atmosphere. Finally, whenever something is perceived, it appears *as something,* it appears *in this way and not in another.* Consequently, symbolic features inhere in the senses and in their spatial organisation from the beginning and do not only arise on a certain level of elaboration. Symbolic aspects belong to what I would call *Urdeutung,* a primary and productive form of interpretation which contrasts with other interpretations, not with something which is purely given. Seeing means *seeing as,* perception includes apperception, and consequently the so-called sense-data are nothing other than artificial constructs. There is a history of colour and sound perception whose traces can be discovered down to the neuro-physiological level. Selections which take place in the various fields of the senses provoke conflicts between divergent sense interpretations, and they produce deep contrasts like that between one culture in which the eye is predominant and another that gives preference to the ear. Although phenomenologists generally do not focus their research primarily on historical details, they have to consider the fact that every sense organisation and every space organisation is submitted to a process of normalisation. As Husserl suggests, *aisthesis* itself is divided into *ortho-aisthesis* and *hetero-aisthesis.* This assumption is not so far from Foucault's reference to *heterotopics.*[9]

Actual, Habitual, and Virtual Space

Our body movements are not restricted to momentary situations, they are deeply embedded into time processes and into the history of our body. Our *actual* body condenses into a *habitual* body whose limbs function as guards of the past (*gardiens du passé*). Proust readers will remember the initial passage of the *Recherche* where the narrator minutely describes the embarrassment of somebody who wakes up in the foreign environment of a hotel room. It would be a real disaster if absent-mindedness were doubled by an "absent-bodyness"! Moreover, our body becomes enlarged by a *virtual* body which opens a range of possibilities. Such time-dependent structures, pervading our bodily existence through and through, do not exclude considerable variation of the import of past and future and the roles of repetition and innovation from one situation or from one individual, one group and one culture to the other. To be as original as possible should not be taken as a universal or even categorical imperative. Normality allows for great variability. But it degenerates to pathological deformations when either the sense of reality (*Wirklichkeitssinn*) or Musil's sense of possibility (*Möglichkeitssinn*) reaches an extreme point. Such extremes may be illustrated by the heterogeneous behaviour of two patients to whom the psychopathologist Eugène Minkowski (1968, p. 257) posed the simple question: "Where are you?" The one patient, a paralytic, answered by pointing to the place where he was then standing whereas the other, a schizophrenic, declared: "I know where I am, but I do not feel that I am there." Or we could again mention Kurt Goldstein's famous patient Schneider. Suffering from the after-effects of a brain injury he remains capable of grasping his nose when bitten by a gnat, but is not able to perform the symbolic act of pointing to it.[10] At this point we encounter another suture of experience, this time connecting doing and knowing.

Regarded from a wider perspective we can observe that experience, when it loses balance, tends either towards *reality without open possibilities* or towards *virtuality without anchorage in reality*, and we further notice that our body presents itself as a scene on which such alternatives are displayed in an experimental or in a pathological manner. It seems to me that today, under the increasing influence of high technology, the process of over-emphasising virtuality largely prevails against the more traditional manner of overemphasising actuality. In this respect we can re-consider Cervantes' famous pair Don Quixote and Sancho Pansa: the master living in the heaven of chivalrous tales, fighting windmills, the servant standing with both feet on the ground of every-day reality. The eccentricity of Don Quixote would be a striking example for the survival of a vanishing reality or for what Merleau-Ponty (1945, p. 99, Engl. 109) calls the "scholastics of existence."[11] Clinging to reality at any price turns into fiction, and an over-embodiment produces specific forms of disembodiment.

Being in Place and out of Place

In Lecture V on the selfhood and otherness of our body, we came across a strange process of self-doubling. In this context we pointed to the fact that the German language allows us to render this status with the double term *Leib-Körper.* As has been shown, this sort of doubling is not restricted to extraordinary events, it belongs to our precarious position in the world, including our living in space and time. Bound to my operative body, I remain *here* and *now,* just at the zero point of our field of experience from which different co-ordinates rise. However I simultaneously find myself *anywhere* in the world, due to the fact that my own "here" and "now" as well as your or our common "here" and "now" can be transformed and, to some extent, have already been transformed into local and temporal data. The basic, unreachable and immemorial fact that I was born, notwithstanding its singularity, finds its place on our geographical maps and in our calendars in terms of a certain place and date of birth. The fact that the way in which this transformation is performed differs from culture to culture, and that in this process fantastic legends or historical documents play different roles, does not exclude the fact that this singular event leaves its traces, even its statistical dry sand in the world of facts. Or take another example, the incursion of scientific inventions. From time to time something happens which disturbs our personal or our cultural time-table, surprising us in a good or bad manner, but even in this case something will be registered e.g. the fact that Roentgen discovered x-rays in his Würzburg laboratory on November 8, 1895. Even the protagonists of the French revolution, who were convinced that they were founding a new era, performed their work around the Louvre and the Bastille, following the rhythm of day and night, of spring and fall. Similar things hold true for making contracts; contracts happen here and now, not anywhere, and to some extent they always interrupt the course of things. Nevertheless they get recorded, witnessed and signed — as if, while writing one's own name, one were to look over one's own shoulders and at one's own fingers. A person who argues that our use of watches, calendars and maps is inauthentic because it only touches something *on* me or *on* you, leaving my- or yourself aside, would fall into bad faith — unless one were to stop talking about oneself, helping oneself, reminding oneself, making agreements, playing chess or *go*, taking part in festivals etc. In short, unless one were to stop living *leibhaftig*: in flesh and blood, *en chair et en os.* Just as our body, assuming some features of a social body and of a physical thing, itself becomes a part of the world which it opens and articulates, in just the same way our original here and now becomes a part of the situation it inaugurates and maintains. System theorists call this re-entry; the process of drawing distinctions, by which the world becomes ordered, can itself be observed as something to be distinguished, but making distinctions and observing them never coincide. There always remains a blind spot, something invisible within the visible, which can be shown but not abolished.[12]

In order to highlight the paradox of being in time and space and simultaneously being out of it, let us finally consider the zero point of traditional topologies and chronologies. Where is the so-called navel of the world? If there were something like the centre of the world we could not locate it within the world without referring to it. Or take initial events like the foundation of Rome, the destruction of the Jewish temple, the birth of Christ or Buddha, the enthronement of a new emperor: in what year did they happen? We can answer these questions only in a paradoxical or tautological way. Rome was founded in the very year in which Rome was founded, Christ was born in the very year in which Christ was born, the emperor was enthroned in the first year of his reign, and so on. In a certain sense, all that is very common. Where is here? It is precisely where somebody who says "here" is standing. And when is now? Now is just the moment when somebody says "now." The rest is splitting concepts as in the chapter on "Sensory certitude" in Hegel's

Phenomenology of the Spirit where indexical expressions like "here" and "today" are treated as predicates, with the effect that our bodily existence functions only as a spring-board.

Husserl, who was no greater a friend of paradoxes than Russell was, tackles the problem in his own manner in his *Crisis* (Hua VI, §§ 53 f.). He starts from the fact that the transcendental *subject for the world* finds itself at the same time as an *object in the world.* In order to overcome the paradoxical situation that "the subjective part of the world swallows up, so to speak, the whole and thus itself too," he claims that the subject constitutes itself as an object. This process of self-objectivation or mundanisation includes acts of self-temporisation and self-spatialization. But we know to what extent the riddles of self-constitution i.e. the constitution of the self-object by the self-subject, pursued Husserl. The central question of otherness which he tried to solve by referring to a sort of de-presentation (*Ent-Gegenwärtigung*) and of self-alienation (*Ent-Fremdung*) (Hua VI, 189, Engl. 185) functions as a permanent trouble spot because of the gaps permanently opening within the experience of my own self and within that of the Other. But the problem can be exposed in more general terms, close to the Cartesian counter-position based on the duality of *res cogitans* and *res extensa.* The paradox mentioned will vanish as soon as we suppose two different sorts of being, on the one hand somebody seeing from *nowhere,* as somebody who *sees without being seen,* on the other hand something located *anywhere,* as something which *is seen without seeing for its part.* By contrast, the paradox blossoms when we presuppose some-body who both *sees and is seen,* and this in terms of a self-doubling process, characterised by Merleau-Ponty (1964b p. 165 f., Engl. p. 124 f.) as a "non-coincidence" or as a "coincidence from afar," by Plessner as an "eccentric positionality" (see above p. 71). We are standing, so to speak, beside ourselves. Similar paradoxes could be made out in the spheres of hearing, touching, moving or speaking as we showed in our earlier lecture on the body.

Globalisation, Localisation and Beyond

The original fissure which separates the self from itself continues in terms of a "fissure of being" (Merleau-Ponty 1964b, pp. 96, 289, Engl. 235). It encroaches on the world, on the time and the place in which we live. The place from where the whole of reality unfolds its possibilities does not find its place within the whole — unless we "forget" what we are doing here and now, when responding to concrete situations and meeting with actual challenges. The oblivion of one's own involvement in what is going on in the world induces a *double jeu.* We pretend that we could simultaneously hold our own position and draw upon the whole. Being here at a certain place, we nevertheless lay claim to divine omnipresence.

This double game seems to belong to the modern Western tradition which tries, in vain I would say, to reconcile the changing perspectives of particular subjects with the universal claim of one and the same reason. This project must fail because the point of view of universality does not allow for a universal point of view (see Lecture II on the Third Party). However, what is to be found today are splinters — some call it post-modernity. Concerning our special question of being here in the world, one could speak of a quarrel between globalists and localists which reminds us, to some extent, of the 18th century's *Querelles des anciens et des modernes.* As it is often the case, both parties have their good points. On the one hand, globalisation opens frontiers and extends horizons. Networks multiply connections. Code switching enhances flexibility. In consequence of the acceleration of communication by electronic media we are not only up to date, but also so to speak up to place. This process of globalisation crosses the borders of the various subsystems. It affects the economic exchange of goods, the cultural exchange of ideas, and it does not come to a stop in front of politics, rights and morals, opening the perspective of a "world democracy." The electronic network makes it more difficult for dictators to keep their country closed and to exclude the public from what they are doing. In 1968 in Prague the Russian tanks had to advance in the light of film cameras. But on the other hand, those who defend local restrictions shield limited forms of life, arguing that they cannot be extended in infinitum without losing their contours.[13] They will insist on the fact that there is no connection (*Anschluß*) without exclusion (*Ausschluß*), that there is no information without deformation, and that, in opposition to globalistic slogans evoking a technological version of the traditional "all together" (ὁμοῦ πάντα), the media fight each other in their daily struggle for our attention. So the users of networks do not behave like mere spiders in the web, doing their peaceful work. Localists will oppose the levelling of all things which even goes to the extent that hard cash, the *klingende Münze* that can be handled, is changed into anonymous electronic processes. Against rash wear and tear they can defend the meandering of sense. Should we expect the truth to lie in the middle as a golden mean, as an *aurea mediocritas*? But where could we find such a centre, such a *Mittelpunkt*?

In some respects globalisation appears to be something rather old. From Parmenides' sphere of Being up to Hegel's dialectics as a circle of circles, thinking has been always tempted by figures in which every point has the same distance to the centre. And such a thinking always provided for some practical orientation. The cosmic orders from which our reflections started used to have a concentric shape. By contrast, modernity stands for a certain decentring which finds its resonance in seismographic authors like Pascal, who evokes infinite spaces that ignore us, and the abyss (*gouffre*) opening under our feet, or in Nietzsche's cosmo-theological visions, where the earth wanders through the universe, untied from its sun (*Gay Science*, aph. 125, KSA, vol. 3, p. 481). But even a sober author like Kant, discussing the *Conjectural Beginning of Human History* (ed. Weischedel, vol. VI, p. 89), does not hesitate to depict the situation of humans as that of beings standing "on the margin of an abyss, filled with infinite possibilities."

If we continue to regard this situation in the light of the bodily "here," we stumble over two reactions which are diametrically opposed. They correspond to what I shall call *globalism* and *localism*, in order to suggest that in both cases certain trends are forced to an extreme. Globalists fly forwards, adhering to a mere technological progress. The centre shifts into the future. This sort of globalism could be classified as an offshoot of a certain Western rationality. "Here" manifests itself as a shifting term, oscillating between everywhere and anywhere. The technical omnipresence of a super-net, which — as Marx would have said — still has its "theological snags," leads to the levelling of being here or there, to the devitalisation of the Here. Space approximates a sort of "space without qualities." On the other hand, localism also proves to be an offshoot. Reacting to the volatilisation of the Here, it ends with a fixation on Here. Yielding to an anti-technical form of regress, one clings to what one had or, to put it in more apt terms, to what one believes one had. Space without qualities turns into a space with fixed qualities. If we remember ideologies such as that of blood and soil

(*Blut und Boden*) we can see to what extent an excessive attachment to one's own soil contributes to transforming strangers into enemies.

However our phenomenological description of space and body leads us beyond these dubious alternatives and extremes. When we really take notice of our situation in the world, we become aware that the "here" which marks our position has certain features of a "not-here." The place or *Topos* of our experience shows certain aspects of a not-place, of an *Atopia*. We have never been and will never be completely at home in the world, and this applies in clear opposition to traditional concentric orders, widening from the narrowness of a home-world to a world home e. g. from the *oikos* through the *polis* to a sort of *cosmopolis*. As we have shown, the life-world itself splits into *home-world* and *alien world* (*Heimwelt / Fremdwelt*). Such a splitting is not fatal. On the contrary it asks for *hospitality* and allows it, preparing the ground for an ethics of dwelling with others in the world. The internal doubling of the world we have in mind has nothing to do with the idols that Nietzsche tries to unmask, it is far from duplicating our world in a back world (*Hinterwelt*) or in another world beyond this world. World-orders and life-forms, being limited, do *not* point to *another world*, they rather point to our world *as another*. Whatever presents itself as ordinary, be it our corporeality, our language or our actions, has its own outside, its own beyond. It may suffice to call to mind that the different attempts made by Merleau-Ponty, Levinas or Foucault aim at a new kind of exterior which is not derived from a Hegelian process of self-exteriorisation.

Because the operations of our body by far precede and exceed their thematization, we never totally know where we are. When we pose the question "Where am I? Where are we?" we start from *elsewhere*. The blind spot mentioned above does not only affect our perception and our consciousness, marking a sort of imperception in the heart of our perception, a sort of unconsciousness in the heart of our consciousness, it also affects our being here and now. There is an *alien topos* (*xenos topos*) underlying our *own* or *proper topos* (*oikeios topos*). This *atopia*, this not-place, ascribed to the Platonic Socrates, opens the door to an open series of *heterotopias* (see Foucault 1994).[14] There are different ways to be here, even on the historical and cultural level. Due to these blind spots and variations, our being here and now will never be registered once and for all by a cosmological or historical world atlas and by a cosmological or historical calendar. Corresponding to the well-known time-lag (*Zeitverschiebung*) we experience when we fly from one continent to another, there is a specific *space-lag* (*Ortsverschiebung*). We always come back to ourselves, being at once here and elsewhere. Hence the famous definition of the human being in terms of reason and language, the *logos*, has to be complemented and modified by certain features of *topos*. After all, we have to recognise that, owing to this self-distance, we come closer to other times and other places and closer to the times and places of others than by clinging to fantastic and often violent ideals orientated on a universal survey or a universal communication. Thus our phenomenology of body and space takes on features of a sort of xenology which prevents us from simply revolving around ourselves.

Notes

Preface

1. See *Acts of the Apostles*. 2, 6.

Lecture I: Experience of the Other

1. See the publication of the remarks on Frazer in Wittgenstein, *Philosophical Occasions* (1993), pp. 123–125.
2. More about this is to be found in Julia Kristeva, *Strangers to Ourselves* (1988, Engl. 1991).
3. See René Spitz, *The First Year of Life* (1965). On page 104 he quotes from Virgil's *Aeneid*: "Incipe, parve puer, risu cognoscere matrem!"
4. The Latin word *domesticare* (= to tame) is derived from *domus* (= house).
5. More about this in my paper "Das Phänomen des Fremden und seine Spuren in der klassischen griechischen Philosophie" (2001).
6. It would be interesting to compare this double way of waging war with Sun Zi's classical book on *Making War*, written only a few decades earlier than Plato's *Republic*. What the Chinese author praises as the finest of the finest is the ability "to make the will (to fight) of (hostile) people wither away without fighting." So even in time of war, violence is permanently questioned and withdrawn instead of being legitimated or simply committed. We shall come back to this issue in lecture VI.
7. "Savage" or "sauvage" goes back to *silva* (= forest) or *silvestris* (= belonging to the forest), whereas the corresponding Greek word ἄγριος refers to ἄγρος (= field or *Acker*), denoting people who live and work in the fields, *auf dem Land*. These environmental connotations indicate how denotations can turn into devaluation. Even the *Communist Manifesto* still evokes the "Idiotismus des Landlebens" i.e. the "idiocy of country life."
8. Traditional label used for socialists during the German Empire, when in Europe the adherence to one's own nation had quasi-religious features.
9. Under this title I have tried to give a diagnosis of our time, highly

stimulated by the motive of alienness. See *Die Verfremdung der Moderne* (2001).

10. From the etymological point of view it should be noted that *foreign* goes back to the Latin word *foris* (= outside, out of doors, abroad), whereas *stranger* and *étranger* are derived from the Latin word *extraneus* (= being outside). The Greek word ξένον is more closely connected with the third aspect of strangeness.
11. See the Adorno's essay "Wörter aus der Fremde" in: *Noten zur Literatur II* (1961). Adorno defends the productive effects of foreign words against any form of *Deutschtümelei*.
12. In French there is the word *autrui* which exclusively refers to somebody like me; close to it is the word *altérité* which is reserved to the otherness of the Other. The rather worn out term *différence* shares its ambiguity with the English word *otherness*. In the end, the main point depends on the use of the terms and not on their general definition.
13. Let me mention that Husserl continually uses terms like *Fremdheit*, *Fremderfahrung*, *Fremdich*, *Fremdleib* or *Fremdwelt*, and that in our everyday language we speak of *Fremdsprache*, *Orts-* and *Landesfremder*, *Fremde* and so on. This does not mean that it is easy to say what all these forms of *Fremdheit* really mean.
14. It may be that this peculiar experience of what is absent or remote, something completely different from any kind of negative predication, can be related to the Chinese concept of "nothingness" (無, *wu*), which clearly contrasts with the negation particle "not" (不, *bu*) in evoking the experience of stillness, darkness or emptiness.
15. It would be grammatically and philosophically correct to say either "I am another" or "Me is another."
16. See the text "Oriental Aesthetics and Modern Art" (1992), quoted from the Catalogue *Liu Guo Song*, Hong Kong Museum of Art, 2004, p. 114. The painter makes a truth of his motto, transforming Chinese landscapes into moon landscapes and into colour craters and, on the other hand, providing Western informal painting with a cosmological background. In his oeuvre he tries to avoid two extremes, both of which are hostile to what he has in mind: "We are neither ancient Chinese nor modern Westerners. If copying ancient Chinese paintings is forgery, so is producing modern Western paintings. Imitating the new of the West is no substitute for imitating the old of the Chinese. As a modern Chinese painter aspiring to create, one has to deliver a new kind of painting that has never been seen in the East or West, and which is unique to China." From "The Way of Chinese Modern Painting" (1965), ibid., p. 104.
17. See Leibniz' famous question "Why is there being rather than (*plutôt*) nothing?"

18. I shall repeatedly refer to the motive of *Gleichsetzen des Nichtgleichen* which Nietzsche exposes with particular clarity in his early essay *Von Wahrheit und Lüge im außermoralischen Sinne* (KSA, vol. 1, p. 880) and which has been in my mind like a motto since I first used it in *Ordnung im Zwielicht*, p. 93, Engl. p. 56.
19. Instead of saying something is all right or okay we say in German: *etwas ist in Ordnung*. Such phrases are certainly not as empty as they seem to be; they involve a lot of everyday philosophy.
20. See Freud's essay *Das Unheimliche* dating from 1919.
21. I refer to Ilya Prigogine's and Isabelle Stenger's attempt to establish a dialogue with nature, starting from new trends in the natural sciences and in philosophy: *Dialog mit der Natur* (1986), Engl.: *Order out of Chaos* (1984).
22. Certainly this is not the only way to centre the world around one's own culture. It is quite possible to adhere to a sort of cosmocentrism up to the point where the order of one's own life blends into an all-embracing order of Nature and where a certain kingdom is promoted to the rank of a Middle Kingdom.
23. On Husserl's *Ineinander* see e.g. *Crisis*, Hua VI, pp. 257–260, English pp. 254–257. Elias, who did his doctorate with Husserl before turning to sociology, uses the term *Verflechtung* in his paper "*Die Gesellschaft der Individuen*," written in 1939, re-published in Elias 1987. Merleau-Ponty was also inspired by Husserl when he developed his idea of the *entrelacs* or *entrelacement* (see *The Visible and the Invisible*, 1964, pp. 74, 172 ff., Engl. pp. 130ff), but also by Valéry when he enriched this idea with the optical term *chiasma*, which literally means the crossing of the optical nerves (see ibid., p. 268, Engl. p. 214 and *Signs*, p. 294, Engl. p. 231). More about the whole problematic in *Antwortregister*, Part III, ch. 8: "Ineinander von Eigenem und Fremdem" and in *Topographie des Fremden*, ch. 3: "Verschränkung von Heimwelt und Fremdwelt."
24. See Iris Därmann and Christoph Jamme, eds., *Fremderfahrung und Repräsentation* (2002).
25. In French: "Quand on veut étudier les hommes, il faut regarder près de soi; mais pour étudier l'homme il faut apprendre à porter sa vue au loin; il faut d'abord observer les différences pour découvrir les propriétés."

Lecture II: Response to the Other

1. Quoted from *Shorter Novels* of Herbert Melville (1942).
2. Whereas intentionality corresponds to what I call comprehensive order (*Gesamtordnung*), in which everybody and everything participates more or less, regularity refers to a basic order (*Grundordnung*) to which everybody is submitted. The classic model for the first type of order is the cosmos, for

the second it is the tribunal. Further explications are to be found in *Order in the Twilight.*

3. See my references in *Antwortregister*, p. 330. As for Husserl's return to a pre-reflexive and even pre-intentional level, I refer to my remarks in *Das Zwischenreich des Dialogs* (1971), pp. 98–101, 120–124. We might wish that Husserl's departure from "representational thinking" were more distinct and decisive, but this does not mean that a corresponding change in his thought did not occur.
4. Cf. e.g. Hua IV, 336: the impression "*in der Weise eines ichfremd Affizierenden*"; Hua X, 88: to receive in a passive manner "*Neues, Fremdes, Originäres*"; Hua XV, 128: hyletic elements as so to speak "*Ichfremdes.*"
5. The attempt to think of self-affection as pure immediacy of life leads to a dead end in my opinion. The negative characterisation of self-affection as non-intentional, non-representational, non-seeing, or non-ecstatic constantly refers to a world-reference which it suspends. On the other hand, a positive characterisation, trying to begin immediately with the self-reference of life, would contradict itself, since all words which give voice to something differentiate themselves from that to which they give voice — unless life were to realise the miracle of expressing itself or better of expressing itself in silence in a "discourse of life" (cf. M. Henry, *Phénoménologie matérielle*, 1990, p. 131). For the way out of the dilemma, mentioned in point (3), cf. in more detail: *Antwortregister*, Part II, ch. 3.
6. Cf. Husserl's third volume on intersubjectivity, Hua XV, 342, 362.
7. M. Heidegger, *Beiträge zur Philosophie*, in GA 65 (1989), p. 161. But already in *Sein und Zeit* (p. 137, Engl. p. 176.) Heidegger uses the simple word *Angänglichkeit* in order to denote something which touches me, comes across to me.
8. Sartre's simple statement: "On ne constitue pas autrui, on le rencontre" (*L'être et le néant*, p. 307) proves to be true, but differently than the author thought.
9. Neglecting the responsive difference by transforming the to-which (*Worauf*) of the response into the what (*Was*) of predication has a long tradition. This tradition can be traced back to Aristotle's doctrine of categories where primacy is given to οὐσία, the so-called substance. In his perceptive comment, based on Benveniste's linguistic analysis, Tze-wan Kwan (1995, pp. 256–260) shows that the first category, as well as some others, is derived from interrogative words such as "what," "how much," "where," etc. which are all used in our everyday language. However, all questions introduced by these interrogative words are related to *what is said*, not to the very *event of saying*, which permanently exceeds what is said simply by responding to what has to be said. Concerning the doubling of speech into the saying and the said see lecture IV.

10. Cf. my essay on Nietzsche "Der blinde Fleck der Moral" in *Deutsch-Französische Gedankengänge.*
11. See Joseph Weizenbaum's report on the Computer ELIZA, which was trained to play a psychotherapist or, to put it more aptly, to parody one. The answers which the computer gives are more appropriate the more stereotypical the questions are which the human partner poses (*Computer Power and Human Reason,* 1976, introduction).
12. Cf. Goldstein, Kurt, *Der Aufbau des Organismus,* Den Haag: M. Nijhoff, 1934, pp. 265–282; English, pp. 427–450. On the origin of these key concepts, which I use in my own way, see *Antwortregister,* pp. 457–459.
13. Cf. my essay on Levinas "Singularität im Plural" in *Deutsch-Französische Gedankengänge.*
14. See *Conflict of the Faculties,* Second Part, sect. 7, Weischedel, vol. VI, p. 361.
15. Using the possibility operator P, the proposition "It is necessary that p" ("N p") can be translated as "not P (not p)."
16. See Derrida's paper "Freud and the Scene of Writing" in *Writing and Difference.*
17. See Thomas Bedorf's monograph *Dimensionen des Dritten* (2003) which confronts various authors such as Simmel, Freud, Lacan, Sartre and Levinas with each other.
18. *Écrits* (1966), p. 287. Lacan alludes to the well-known liturgical formula *In nomine patris et filio et spiritus sancti.*
19. Cf. my paper "The Paradox of Expression" (2000).

Lecture III: The Power of Events

1. Quoted in this chapter simply by page numbers.
2. Nietzsche would have been one of them, but his philosophical hour came later; much the same can be said about Kierkegaard.
3. In what follows I shall only sharpen what I have extensively discussed elsewhere. See especially: *Ordnung im Zwielicht,* Engl. *Order in the Twilight:* ch. A, 8–10 (Engl. ch. I, 8–10): intermediary events, and ch. E, 5 (Engl. ch. 5, 5): key events; *Antwortregister:* Part II, ch. 2–3: the event of saying, and recently *Bruchlinien der Erfahrung,* where the diastasis between pathos and response permanently leads us along the tracks of event thinking.
4. The distinction between neptunists and vulcanists dates from the age of Goethe. Chinese readers may remember Lao Zi writing in his *Dao De Jing:* "All over the world there is nothing more soft and more weak than water. But still nothing equals it for how it harasses the hard." Or to put it in the words of Bertold Brecht, the German poet who learned from the Chinese sages: "Daß das weiche Wasser in Bewegung / Mit der Zeit den mächtigen Stein besiegt./ Du verstehst, das Harte unterliegt." ("Legende von der Entstehung des Buches Taoteking auf dem Weg des Laotse in die

Emigration," written in 1938). One should also take note of the fact that Lao Zi presents water as a "feminine element," appealing to a gendered Nature, as most archaic cosmologies do.

5. Together with Montaigne, Pascal is one of the early authors who, starting from the corporeal constitution of human beings, developed a sense for what happens to us and provokes us before we behave as the master and the owner of outer and inner nature. Concerning the pre-history of this debate see the article "Impersonalien" in *Historisches Wörterbuch der Philosophie*, vol. 4. The so-called impersonal expressions give event thinking a linguistic background which may preserve it from some speculative flights of fancy.
6. See Georg Christoph Lichtenberg, *Sudelhefte* (1975), pp. 412: "*Es denkt*, sollte man sagen, so wie man sagt: *es blitzt*. Zu sagen *cogito*, ist schon zu viel, so bald man es durch *Ich denke* übersetzt. Das *Ich* anzunehmen, zu postulieren, ist praktisches Bedürfnis"; in this connection see Nietzsche, *Jenseits von Gut und Böse*, 1. Hauptstück, Aph. 17, KSA, vol. 5, p. 31: "*Es* denkt: aber dafl dies 'es' gerade jenes alte berühmte 'Ich' sei, ist, milde geredet, nur eine Annahme, eine Behauptung, vor allem keine 'unmittelbare Gewiflheit'. Zuletzt ist schon mit diesem 'es denkt' zuviel getan: schon dies 'es' enthält eine Auslegung des Vorgangs und gehört nicht zum Vorgange selbst."
7. *Phenomenology of Perception*: "On perçoit en moi, ce n'est pas moi qui perçoit" p. 249, Engl. 215: "[...] that *one* perceives in me, and not that *I* perceive."
8. *Se una notte d'inverno un viaggiatore*, 1979, p. 176, Engl. p. 176: One should say "it thinks" (*pensa*) in the same way as one says "it is raining" (*piove*), and correspondingly: "I read, therefore *it* writes," "Io leggo dunque *esso* scrive."
9. See also the middle voice in Greek grammar which is located between active and passive. Émile Benveniste (1966, p. 172, Engl. p. 149) comments on this as follows: "the subject is the centre as well as the agent of the process; he achieves something which is being achieved in him — being born, sleeping, lying, imagining, growing, etc. He is indeed inside the process of which he is the agent." The author makes a great effort to overcome the simple opposition between activity and passivity; however he still adheres to traditional categories such as subject, agent and inside, and does not go far enough to revise them in the light of what is happening.
10. I refer to Tze-wan Kwan's highly interesting paper on "Wilhelm von Humboldt on the Chinese language" (2001), p. 189. I would like to add some special remarks. First, in his *Phenomenology of Perception* (1945, pp. 309–324, Engl. pp. 267–280) Merleau-Ponty discusses the possibility of perceiving movements without supposing something which is moved. He draws on corresponding experiments carried out by the Gestalt psychologist Max Wertheimer. In this case we lack an appropriate grammar

to describe what we see. Secondly, on the first page of *The Order of Things* Foucault mentions Borges' "Chinese Encyclopaedia" which registers animals as follows: "a) belonging to the Emperor, b) embalmed, c) domesticated, d) young pigs, e) sirens, f) fabulous, g) dogs set free, h) included in the present classification, i) behaving like fools, j) innumerable, k) drawn with a very fine brush of camel hair, l) et cetera, m) which just broke the jug, n) which seen from afar resemble flies." He takes this amusing bestiary as a sort of surrealistic experiment which can scatter orders by introducing some unusual herotopias. But he seems not to take notice of the heterogeneous potential dormant in the very structure of the Chinese language. One could argue that in a language which uses words without inflection (vocalic change, prefixes, suffixes or sound reduplication) i.e. without being able to move, so to speak, on the spot, each word is much more movable, seeking hold on other words. On this linguistic peculiarity, see Kwan 2001, p. 193 f. The author refers to Humboldt who clearly distinguishes between highly inflective languages such as Sanskrit and its successors which prefer morphological forms, and languages such as Chinese which, inasmuch as they lack such forms of inflection, emphasise syntax as a kind of "word order." He highlights Humboldt's effort to balance achievements and shortcomings between different types of language without privileging one of them. Such a linguistic comparison takes place against a background of a mutual alienness which will never be neutralised or overcome from the position of a Third Party.

11. The "Buddhist Truth of Suffering" seems to be a special sort of or "key" primary passion: "Birth is suffering; decay is suffering; death is suffering; grief and lamentation, pain, misery and tribulation are sufferings; it is a suffering not to get what is desired ..." This Buddhist text is quoted from Kwan 1995, p. 286. It leads us to the abysses of primal experiences which vary from one culture or religion to another, but not without some mutual resonance. The corresponding intercultural cross-studies are also "comparing the incomparable" (Levinas 1974, p. 202).
12. See Maurice Blanchot: *L'entretien infini* (1969), especially p. 106 ff.: "L'interruption."
13. Jean Laplanche, *La révolution copernicienne inachevée* (1992), p. 396. This author has developed a psychoanalysis based on the primacy of the Other whose main orientation converges with my own attempts in many ways; this includes the judgement about what happens to us.

Lecture IV: Time-Lag

1. Cf. Paul Ricœur's interpretation of the time novel in the second volume of his great work *Temps et récit*, Engl. *Time and Narration.*

2. On Merleau-Ponty's conception of time see the essay "Wirbel der Zeit," which I have written with Regula Giuliani, see *Idiome des Denkens. Deutsch-Französische Gedankengänge II*, Frankfurt am Main: Suhrkamp. 2005.
3. Cf. *De interpretatione* 3, 16b6: 'Ρῆμα δέ ἐστι τὸ τροσσαημαῖνον χρόνον.
4. When in what follows I use the word flesh along with the common word body, I do so in the same sense as the later Merleau-Ponty speaks of *chair* in order to emphasise the material and textural character of our body which corresponds to a certain "flesh," to a certain *Leibhaftigkeit* of the things, of the world and even of language and time. See *The Visible and the Invisible*, 1964, p. 150, Engl. p. 111f. : "Sous la solidité de l'essence et de l'idée, il y a le tissu de l'expérience, cette chair du temps [...]"
5. For more on this, see ch. 3 of my work *Sinnesschwellen*.
6. On the responsive character of forgetting and remembering, which in the following section also proves extremely relevant, cf. my book *Antwortregister*, Part III, ch. 5.
7. Cf. Emmanuel Levinas, *Otherwise than Being or beyond Essence*, passim.
8. Concerning A. Schütz, *Collected Papers*, vol. I, pp. 11–12 and p. 147 with respect to Husserl. In Piaget's epistemology the term "reversibility" is used to define an internal act which can be achieved in the opposite direction, be it as negation or as reciprocity. Being capable of carrying out this operation indicates that somebody has reached the stage of full rationality. This over-rationalisation was strongly critisised by Merleau-Ponty in his Sorbonne Lectures. See also, from the pedagogical point of view, Käte Meyer-Drawe, *Leiblichkeit und Sozialität* (1984).
9. Husserl already spoke of retention and perception as being "differently timed (*verschiedenzeitig*)" (Hua X, 205).
10. That means that the "standing now" gives way to a "distant" or "differing now," in agreement with what we call diastase.

Lecture V: Bodily Experience between Selfhood and Otherness

1. In Japanese: *Tanin no Kar*, we quote from the English translation (1967), pp. 12–15.
2. As we all know the history of technology did not stop here. Elsewhere I have tried to show how phenomenology includes a genuine sort of phenomeno-technic. See *Bruchlinien der Erfahrung* (2002), chap. VIII. Concerning the role of the body in the development of human skills I refer to the rich resource of documents presented by the French palaeontologist André Leroi-Gourhan in *Gesture and Speech* (1993).
3. In contrast to this, the Chinese word *shen* (身) first of all suggests a living body. Interpretations of the pictorial aspect of the ideogram oscillate between the reference to a fat man (attribute of wealth and also allusion to Buddha) and a pregnant wife; obviously, both referents are full of life.

4. Cf. e. g. *Crisis*, § 28; the American translator renders *Leib* and *Körper* as "living body" and "physical body" respectively.
5. *Also sprach Zarathustra*: "Von den Verächtern des Leibes," KSA, vol. 4, p. 39.
6. See Helmuth Plessner, *Die Stufen des Organischen und der Mensch* (1981), p. 367, concerning the double aspect of our human existence as *Leib* and as *Körper*, and *Conditio Humana* (1983), p. 190, concerning our human existence as *leibhaftes Körpersein* and *Körperhaben*. The important book on the *Stufen des Organischen*, in which the author largely draws upon the biological research of his time, was first published in 1928.
7. *Also sprach Zarathustra*: "Von den Verächtern des Leibes," KSA, vol. 4, p. 39 f.
8. This also holds true for the work of language, which takes a specific form in languages in which pictographic and phonetic elements are combined. To give some simple examples, the Chinese equivalents for "water" or "mountain," whose pictograms evoke the rhythm of waves (水) and the rising of mountain peaks (山), obviously make things appear in a certain way. It is only under this condition that it becomes plausible that the combination of "man" (人) and "mountain" (山) results in the complex meaning "immortal" (仙), which clearly differs from Western words like ἀθάνατος or "immortalis" in that it is not based on negation. I do not intend to indulge in wild speculation, I only want to suggest that language contributes in multiple ways to the production and not only to the reproduction of sense, or to say it in German, it contributes to the *Gebung* and not only to the *Wiedergabe* of sense.
9. On self-affection and hetero-affection in Husserl see Dan Zahavi, *Self-Awareness and Alterity* (1999), ch. 7.
10. Ch. VII of my book *Bruchlinien der Erfahrung* goes in this direction.
11. That this type of writing is a complicated story should not be denied. But after all, even the process of walking is not as simple as it looks. At any rate, a sort of writing in which the execution of each character makes us run through a series of individual strokes whose sequence is ordered like a melody could well have the effect that the process of writing is less obscured and less absorbed by what is written down. Spoken Chinese shows similar effects, inasmuch as it is dependent on a system of *tones* which contribute to the discrimination of meaning and do not only express a certain mood or emphasis as *intonation* does (see Kwan 2001, p. 198 f.). Perhaps one must assume that performance and performativity and, in connection with them, corporeality, which in Western countries have recently become a dominant issue, have particularly deep roots in the linguistic practice of China and other Eastern countries. The important role played by calligraphy may be explained in a similar way. In this context it is interesting to draw upon a case of linguistic disturbance affecting the capacity to read. In the course of

medical examinations Kurt Goldstein, the neurologist mentioned above, discovered that his patient Schneider was unable to identify the printed letter K with a hand-written K. This deficiency, which was accompanied by similar deficits affecting other forms of behaviour, is generally classified as a form of concretism i.e. as an incapacity to abstract from concrete circumstances and contexts. However it may be that the patient is not simply fixated on the given situation but is also extremely attentive to the mode or, so to speak, to the tone of writing. Indeed, it makes a difference whether a letter is composed step by step out of isolated strokes, or whether it executed in one and the same stroke.

12. The title *Other Minds* is used by analytical authors, for example by J. L. Austin (see his *Collected Papers*).
13. See my essay "Experience of the Alien in Husserl's Phenomenology" (1990), where I try to point out the radicality of Husserl's approach but also its shortcomings.
14. "La nature est pleine de miracles, mais des miracles de raison," see Leibniz' letter to Bossuet from April 18, 1692.
15. In French: "Autrui, un autre semblable, ou peut-être double de moi, c'est le gouffre le plus magnétique – la question la plus renaissante, l'obstacle le plus malin – chose qui seule empêche tout le reste de ne pas se confondre, s'éloigner ensemble. Singe plus qu'imitateur – reflet qui répond, devance, étonne."

Lecture VI: Violence as Violation

1. The German psychiatrist Wolfgang Blankenburg presents this case in his contribution to the *Festschrift* for George Devereux (1984), p. 42 f.
2. Lec, who earned his living as a diplomat, is the author of a series of *Unfrisierte Gedanken* (see first *Mysli nieuczesane,* Kraków, 1959). These are full of enigmatic allusions and full of wit, intended to resist a less witty political regime.
3. Concerning the following reflections see my earlier article "Grenzen der Legitimierung und die Frage nach der Gewalt," which places the emphasis on the issue of the violation of others' claims, referring to such authors as H. Arendt, M. Foucault, M. Merleau-Ponty, E. Levinas and M. Weber. The article has been published in German in: *Der Stachel des Fremden* (1990) and in English in: J. B. Bradly and N. Garver (eds.): *Justice, Law and Violence* (1991).
4. The "before" of the pre-legal or pre-moral claim must not be understood in terms of events located on a temporal line, but rather in terms of a certain precedence (*Vorgängigkeit*) which corresponds to the inner posteriority (*Nachträglichkeit*) of our response, including legal and moral sorts of responding. Responding means being not completely up to date. Most

theories of practice and discourse miss this point because the specific time of speaking and acting is permanently overshadowed by questions of meaning, goals and rules.

5. In this way one may distinguish between different types of collective violence in Bolshevism and Nazism, as certain historians do.
6. The concept of the collective is ambiguous because it comprehends both the organisation of a group (which may be in accordance with private interests) and the symbolical regulations of group membership. The fact that the distinction between private and public itself has historical roots may be passed over in this context.
7. See the discussion of politics and morals in Semprun's novel *What a Beautiful Sunday!* (1982, pp. 208–215).
8. Aristotle, who so strongly emphasises the goal direction of action and the weighing up of practical motives, introduces a class of "mixed actions" which are located between voluntary and involuntary. These hybrid actions are subject to natural or social constraints (such as sea storm or extortion) so that we do what we do not want to do (*Nic. Ethics,* III, 1). In the case of voluntary acts, Aristotle takes into account the reaching of a state (for example drunkenness) and the formation of habits which considerably restrict the range of action (*ibid.*, III, 7). Cf. also Merleau-Ponty's critique of Sartre for confronting individuals with direct actions without considering the refraction of practical projects by collective symbols (*The Adventures of the Dialectic,* ch. V).
9. The proverbial *De mortuis nil nisi bene* should be extended to a stronger *De victimis nil nisi bene.* The two maxims should not be understood as calls for posthumous justification or historical glossing; they only mean that those who have survived should not abuse the defencelessness of the dead by speaking the last word about them.
10. Cf. on this point Merleau-Ponty's lucid and careful rapprochement of phenomenology and structuralism in his article "From Mauss to Lévi-Strauss," in *Signs* (1960, Engl. 1964).
11. See in this context Leonardo's remark in Goethe's *Wilhelm Meister's Years of Apprenticeship* (book 1, ch. 11) which refers to the first meeting with the "nut-brown girl": "A vivid impression is like another wound; one does not feel it when it is suffered. It is only later that it begins to hurt and to fester." Note that in this context Goethe is speaking of an injury *inflicted on the other* which hurts the person *who inflicts* it. This shows a remarkable intertwining of one's own affects and those of the other.
12. Hegel, *Phänomenologie des Geistes,* Meiner, p. 470.
13. Cf. Levinas' dedication of *Otherwise than Being*: "To the memory of those who were closest among the six million assassinated by the National Socialists, and of the millions on millions of all creeds and all nations,

victims of the same hatred of the other man, the same anti-Semitism." Only the second dedication, written in Hebrew, records the names of Levinas' own parents, brothers and parents-in-law.

14. *Ultima ratio* can not only be translated as "last resort" but also as "reason at the end." Concerning "Gewaltsamkeit" as a specific instrument of politics see Max Weber 1976, p. 29.
15. The concept of counter-violence (*Gegengewalt*) is already found in Kant, though with a negative accent. See *On the Common Saying "That may be right in theory but does not work in practice,"* ed. Weischedel, vol. VI, p. 156.
16. When Derrida, in his famous article "Violence and metaphysics" (in *Writing and Difference*) refers to a "transcendental violence," this can only mean that violence *takes part* in the foundation of sense.

Lecture VII: Being Here and Elsewhere

1. Quoted from Stephen Greenblatt, *Marvellous Possessions* (1991), p. 56, followed by the author's comment on the presuppositions and circumstances of this procedure.
2. Concerning the methodical background of the phenomenological approach I refer to chapter 1 of my book *Grenzen der Normalisierung* (1998), where phenomenology is considered step by step from an eidetic, a transcendental and a structural point of view, leading to a special kind of phenomenological estrangement.
3. It is worth mentioning that οἰκεῖος (= proper) has in itself a topical aspect inasmuch as it is derived from οἶκος (= house).
4. See Husserl's last great work, the *Crisis*. A first fragment appeared in Belgrade in 1936 before it was published, completed by other texts, as volume VI of the *Husserliana* (1954, Engl. 1970).
5. In this context the time aspect, explicitly dealt with in Lecture IV, will be largely neglected; a more complete analysis would have to consider the fact that time and space are interwoven.
6. This peculiar sort of orientation provokes further questions about the degree of body-guided individualisation which obviously differs from culture to culture. One may wonder whether such a heliocentric orientation does not presuppose an over-identification with the sun, which in this case functions as a prominent kind of world-body.
7. I refer to my Beijing Lecture "Between Saying and Showing. Reflections on Husserl's Theory of Occasional Expressions" (in German 2003, in Chinese 2004). There I try to show how Husserl's theory of occasional expressions had a strong effect on linguistics. In this context, Roman Jakobson's essay "Shifters, Verbal Categories, and the Russian Verb" (first published in 1957) was very important. Referring, among others, to Husserl and Bühler, the author distinguishes between the reported process (*énoncé*) and the

reporting process (*énonciation*), both mediated by the so-called shifters. Concerning the doubling of speech, which includes the doubling of our bodily self, of time and place, and which plays a crucial role in my reflections on alienness or otherness, see also *Antwortregister*, part II, ch. 2, 3 and 10.

8. The Chinese signs for "over" and "under": (上, 下), making complementary use of horizontal and vertical strokes, alluding to the earth below and the heaven above, clearly *show* the spatial relations which are only *meant* by signs consisting of letters. Similar things could be said about a sign like 口; the Chinese sign for "mouth" circumscribes, stroke by stroke, the mouth as a kind of hole or opening through which something can go in and come out. The fact that, in accordance with Peirce's semiotics, the iconic aspects of the signs are mingled with symbolical and even with indexical aspects does not exclude that *to some extent* we see what we are thinking of and referring to. André Leroi-Gourhan characterises the Chinese language as a "crossing" of ideographic and phonetic elements, and so he attributes to Chinese writing a state of equilibrium which is unique in the history of mankind because it allows for a sufficient degree of exactness without renouncing the flexibility and multidimensionality of pictures. See the section on Chinese writing in *Gesture and Speech* (1993), ch. VI.
9. As to the motives of normality and normalisation in Husserl, cf. especially Hua IV, § 18 and Hua XIII, Text 14. But this problematic is touched on by other authors such as G. Canguilhem, M. Foucault, A. Schutz and also S. Freud. I have discussed this problematic from different points of view in *Grenzen der Normalisierung*. As to the special history of the eye cf. ch. 6: "Anderssehen" in *Sinnesschwellen* (1999).
10. See Kurt Goldstein, *Der Aufbau des Organismus* (1934), p. 149 f., Engl. p. 237 f., and in more detail "Über Zeigen und Greifen" (1931), republished in *Selected Papers/Ausgewählte Schriften* (1971). This pathological disturbance is extensively commented on by Merleau-Ponty in his *Phenomenology of Perception* (1945), p. 120 ff., Engl. 103 ff.
11. The English translation, which renders this as "a sort of abstraction of that existence," misses the point. "Scholastic" in its pejorative sense does not only mean an abstract, but also a fixed and merely repetitive kind of thinking.
12. The insight that the eye does not see itself goes back at least to Schopenhauer. We find it in such different authors as Wittgenstein, Bataille, Merleau-Ponty, Lacan or Luhmann.
13. In his discussion of friendship, Aristotle already remarks that friendship, like love, does not admit of extension in infinitum (see *Nic. Eth.* VIII, 7).
14. See Michel Foucault, preface to *The Order of Things* (1966, p. 9, Engl. p. XVIII): "Les utopies consolent ... Les hétérotopies inquiètent ..."

Literature

Abé, Kobe, *The Face of Another*, trans. E. Dale Saunders, Tokyo: Charles E. Tuttl Comp., 1967.

Anzieu, Didier, *Le Moi-peau*, Paris: Bordas, 1985.

Arendt, Hannah, *On Violence*, London: Allen Lane, 1970. – German: *Macht und Gewalt*, trans. G. Uellenberg, München: Piper, 1970.

——, *Eichmann in Jerusalem*, New York: Viking Press, 1963. – German: *Eichmann in Jerusalem. Ein Bericht von der Banalität des Bösen*, trans. B. Granzow, 9th ed., München: Piper, 1995.

Austin, John Langshaw, "Other Minds" in *Philosophical Papers*, 3rd ed., Oxford: Clarendon Press, 1979.

Bachelard, Gaston, *La poétique de l'espace*, Paris: P.U.F., 1957. – English: *The Poetics of Space*, trans. M. Jolas, New York: Orion Press and Boston, Mass., Beacon Press, 1969.

Bachtin, Michail M., "Das Wort im Roman." In *Die fsthetik des Wortes*, trans. R. Grübel and S. Reese, Frankfurt/M.: Suhrkamp, 1979.

Bakhtin, Mikhail M., "Discourse in the Novel." In *The Dialogical Imagination*, trans. C. Emerson and M. Holquist, Austin: University of Texas Press, 1981.

——, *Art and Answerability: Early Philosophical Essays*, Austin: University of Texas Press, 1990.

Bedorf, Thomas, *Dimensionen des Dritten*, München: W. Fink, 2003.

Benveniste, Émile, *Problèmes de linguistique générale*, vol. I, Paris: Gallimard 1966. – English: *Problems in General Linguistics*, trans. M. E. Meek, Coral Gables: University of Miami Press, 1968.

Blanchot, Maurice, *L'entretien infini*, Paris: Gallimard, 1969. – English *The Infinite Conversation*, trans. S. Hanson, Minneapolis: University of Minnesota Press, 1993.

Blankenburg, Wolfgang, "Ethnopsychiatrie im Inland. Normen-Probleme im Hinblick auf die Kultur- und Subkultur-Bezogenheit psychiatrischer Patienten." In *Curare*, Special vol. 2, 1984, pp. 39–52.

Brady, James B. and Garver, Newton, eds., *Justice, Law and Violence.* Philadelphia: Temple University Press, 1991.

Bühler, Karl, *Sprachtheorie.* Stuttgart/New York 1982. – English: *Theory of Language,* trans. D. F. Goodwin, Amsterdam/Philadelphia: J. Benjamin, 1990.

Calvino, Italo, *Se una notte d'inverno un viaggiatore,* Torino: Einaudi, 1979. – English: *If on a Winter's Night a Traveller,* trans. W. Weaver, New York: Harcourt, Brace, Jovanovich, 1981.

Därmann, Iris and Jamme, Christoph, eds., *Fremderfahrung und Repräsentation,* Weilerswist: Velbrück, 2002.

Davidson, Donald, *Essays on Actions and Events,* Oxford: Clarendon Press, 1980.

Derrida, Jacques, "Violence et métaphysique"; "Freud et la scène de l'écriture." In *idem: L'Ecriture et la différence.* Paris: Seuil, 1967. – English: "Violence and metaphysics"; "Freud and the Scene of Writing." In *Writing and Difference,* trans. A. Bass, London: Routledge & Kegan, 1978.

Elias, Norbert, *Die Gesellschaft der Individuen.* Frankfurt/M.: Suhrkamp, 1987.

Foucault, Michel, *Les mots et les choses,* Paris: Gallimard 1966. – *The Order of Things,* trans. A. Sheridan, London: Tavistock, 1970.

Gadamer, Hans-Georg, *Wahrheit und Methode,* 2nd ed., Tübingen 1965. – English: *Truth and Method,* trans. J. Weinsheimer and J. Cumming, London: Sheed & Ward, ^{2}1989.

Gabelentz, Georg von der, *Chinesische Grammatik,* Halle: VEB Max Niemeyer, 4. Aufl. 1960.

Goldstein, Kurt, *Der Aufbau des Organismus,* Den Haag: M. Nijhoff, 1934. – English: *The Organism. A Holistic Approach to Biology Derived from Pathological Data in Man,* Boston: Beacon Press, 1963.

——, *Selected Papers/Ausgewählte Schriften,* The Hague: M. Nijhoff, 1971.

Greenblatt, Stephen, *Marvellous Possessions,* Oxford: Clarendon Press, 1991.

Habermas, Jürgen, *Erkenntnis und Interesse,* Frankfurt/M.: Suhrkamp, 1973. – English: *Knowledge and Human Interests,* trans. J. Shapiro, Oxford: Polity Press, 1987.

Hegel, Georg Wilhelm Friedrich, *Phänomenologie des Geistes,* 6th ed., Hamburg: Meiner, 1952. – English: *Phenomenology of Spirit,* trans. A. von Miller, Oxford: Clarendon Press, 1970.

Heidegger, Martin, *Sein und Zeit,* Paris: Niemeyer, 7th ed. 1953. – English: *Being and Time,* trans. J. Stambaugh, Albany: State University of New York, 1996.

——, *Beiträge zur Philosophie* (Gesamtausgabe, vol. 65), Frankfurt/M.: Klostermann, 1989.

Henry, Michel, *Phénoménologie matérielle,* Paris: P.U. F., 1990.

Husserl, Edmund, *Husserliana* (Hua), The Hague/Dordrecht: M. Nijhoff/ Kluwer, 1950 ff.

——, *Logical Investigations*, 2 vols., trans. J. N. Findlay, New York: Humanities Press, 1970.

——, *Cartesian Meditations*, trans. D. Cairns, The Hague: M. Nijhoff, 1977(= Hua I).

——, *Ideas Pertaining to a Pure Phenomenology and to a Phenomenological Philosophy*: First Book, trans. F. Kersten, The Hague: M. Nijhoff, 1983 (= Hua III).

——, *Ideas Pertaining to a Pure Phenomenology and to a Phenomenological Philosophy*: Second Book, trans. R. Rojewicz and A. Schuwer, Dordrecht: Kluwer, 1989 (= Hua IV).

——, *The Crisis of European Sciences and transcendental Phenomenology*, trans. D. Carr, Evanston, Ill.: Northwestern University Press, 1970 (= Hua VI).

——, *On the Phenomenology of the Consciousness of Internal Time*, trans. J. B. Brough, Den Haag: M. Nijhoff, 1991 (= Hua X).

——, *Formal and Transcendental Logic*, trans. D. Cairns, The Hague: M. Nijhoff, 1969 (= Hua XVII).

Jakobson, Roman, "Shifters, Verbal Categories, and the Russian Verb." (1957) In *Selected Writings*, vol. II, The Hague: Mouton, 1971.

Kant, Immanuel, *Werke in sechs Bänden*, ed. W. Weischedel, Darmstadt: Wissenschaftliche Buchgesellschaft, 1963–1964.

Kristeva, Julia, *Étrangers à nous-mêmes*, Paris: A. Fayard, 1988. – English: *Strangers to Ourselves*, trans. L. Roudiez, New York: Columbia University Press, 1991.

Kwan, Tze-wan, "The Doctrine of Categories and the Topology of Concern," in *Analecta Husserliana* XLVI (1995), pp. 243–302 (Dordrecht: Kluwer).

——, "Wilhelm von Humboldt on the Chinese Language – Interpretation and Reconstruction," *Journal of Chinese Linguistics*, vol. 29/2 (2001), pp. 169–242 (Berkeley, USA).

Lacan, Jacques, *Écrits*, Paris: Seuil, 1966. – *Écrits: A selection*, trans. A. Sheridon, New York: Norton, 1977.

Ladd, John, "The Idea of Collective Violence." In Brady and Garver 1991.

Laplanche, Jean, *La révolution copernicienne inachevée*, Paris: Aubier, 1992

Leroi-Gourhan, André, *Gesture and Speech*, trans. A. B. Berger, Cambridge, Mass.: MIT Press, 1993.

Levinas Emmanuel, *Autrement qu'être ou au-delà de l'essence*. Den Haag: M. Nijhoff 1974.

—— English: *Otherwise Than Being, or Beyond Essence*, trans. A. Lingis, Den Haag: Nijhoff, 1981.

Lévi-Strauss, Claude, *Anthropologie structurale* II, Paris: Plon, 1962. – English: *Structural Anthropology* II, trans. M. Layton, New York: Basis Books, 1976.

——, "La place de la culture japonaise dans le monde." In *Revue d'esthétique* 18 (1990).

Lichtenberg, Georg Christoph, *Schriften und Briefe*, vol. 2: *Sudelbücher* II, 2nd ed., München: Hanser, 1975.

Liu Guo Song, *A Universe of his Own*, Catalogue, Hong Kong Museum of Art, 2004.

MacPherson, Crawford Brough, *The Political Theory of Possessive Individualism*, Oxford: Clarendon Press, 1962.

Melville, Herbert, *Shorter Novels*, with an introduction by R. Weaver, Liveright Publishing Corp., 1942.

Merleau-Ponty, Maurice, *Phénoménologie de la perception*. Paris: Gallimard, 1945. – English: *Phenomenology of Perception*, trans. C. Smith, London: Routledge & Kegan Paul, 1962.

——, *Les aventures de la dialectique*. Paris: Gallimard, 1955. – English: *Adventures of the Dialectic*, trans. J. Bien, Evanston: Northwestern University Press, 1973.

——, *Signes*. Paris: Gallimard 1960. – English: *Signs*, trans. R. C. McCleary, Evanston: Northwestern University Press, 1964.

——, *L'úil et l'esprit*, Paris: Gallimard 1964 (= 1964a). English: "Eye and Mind." In *The Aesthetics Reader: Philosophy and Painting*, trans. M. B. Smith, Evanston: Northwestern, 1993.

——, *Le visible et l'invisible*, Paris: Gallimard, 1964 (= 1964b). – English: *The Visible and the Invisible*, trans. A. Lingis, Evanston: Northwestern, 1968.

——, *Merleau-Ponty à la Sorbonne. Résumé de cours 1949–1952*, Grenoble: Cynara, 1988.

Meyer-Drawe, Käte, *Leiblichkeit und Sozialität*, München: W. Fink, 1984.

Minkowski, Eugène, *Le temps vécu*, 2nd ed., Paris: d'Artrey, 1933, Neuch,tel: Delachaux and Nieste, 1968. – English: *Lived Time*, trans. N. Metzel, Evanston: Northwestern University Press.

Musil, Robert, *Der Mann ohne Eigenschaften*, Reinbek: Rowohlt, 1978. – English: *The Man without Qualities*, London: Secker & Warburg, 1955.

Novalis, Friedrich, *Schriften*, ed. by Kluckhohn and Samuel, Stuttgart: Kohlhammer, 1960 ff.

Nietzsche, Friedrich, *Kritische Studienausgabe* (KSA), eds. G. Colli and M. Montinari, Berlin: de Gruyter/dtv, 1980.

Paz, Octavio, *The Collected Poems of Octavio Paz 1957–1987*, trans. E. Weinberger, New York: New Directions, 1987.

Plessner, Helmuth, *Die Stufen des Organischen und der Mensch* (Ges. Schriften, vol. IV), Frankfurt/M.: Suhrkamp, 1981.

——, *Conditio Humana* (Ges. Schriften, vol. VIII), Frankfurt/M.: Suhrkamp, 1983.

Prigogine, Ilya and Stengers, Isabelle, *Order out of Chaos: Man's New Dialogue with Nature*, Boulder: New Science Library, 1984. – German: *Dialog mit der Natur*, trans. F. Giese, München/Zürich: Piper, 5th ed. 1986.

Proust, Marcel, *A la recherche du temps perdu*, 3 vols., Paris: Gallimard 1954. – English:

Ricoeur, Paul, *Temps et récit*, 3. vols., Paris: Seuil 1983–1985. – English: *Time and*

Narrative, trans. K. McLaughlin and D. Pellauer, Chicago: Chicago University Press, 1992.

Röttgers, Kurt, *Spuren der Macht*. Freiburg/München: K. Alber, 1990.

Sartre, Jean-Paul, *L'être et le néant*, Paris: Gallimard, 1943. – English: *Being and Nothingness*, trans. H. E. Barnes, London: Routledge, 1995.

Schmidt, Siegfried J., ed., *Gedächtnis*, Frankfurt/M.: Suhrkamp, 1991.

Schutz, Alfred, *Collected Papers*, vol I., The Hague: M. Nijhoff, 1962.

——, "Don Quixote and the Problem of Reality." In *Collected Papers*, vol. II, The Hague: M. Nijhoff, 1964.

Semprun, Jorge, *What a Beautiful Sunday!*, trans. A. Sheridan, San Diego: Harcourt Brace Jovanovich, 1982.

Spitz, René, *The First Year of Life. A Psychoanalytical Study of Normal and Deviant Development of Object Relations*, New York: International Universities Press, 1965.

Straus, Erwin, *Vom Sinn der Sinne*, 2nd ed., Berlin/NewYork/Heidelberg, 1956. – English: *The Primary World of Senses. A Vendication of Sensory Experience*, trans. J. Needleman, New York: Free Press of Glencoe, 1963.

Valéry, Paul, *Cahiers*, 2 vol., Paris: Gallimard, 1973–74.

Virilio, Paul, *La vitesse de libération*, Paris: Galilée, 1995. – German: *Fluchtgeschwindigkeit*, trans. B. Wilczek, München: Hanser, 1996.

Waldenfels, Bernhard, *Das Zwischenreich des Dialogs. Sozialphilosophische Untersuchungen in Abschluß an Edmund Husserl*, Den Haag: M. Nijhoff, 1971.

——, *Ordnung im Zwielicht*. Frankfurt/M.: Suhrkamp, 1987. – English: *Order in the Twilight*, trans. D. J. Parent, Athens: Ohio University Press, 1996.

——, *Der Stachel des Fremden*, Frankfurt/M.: Suhrkamp, 1990.

——, "Experience of the Alien in Husserl's Phenomenology," trans. A. Steinbock. In: *Research in Phenomenology* 20 (1990), pp. 19–33. German: "Erfahrung des Fremden in Husserls Phänomenologie." In Waldenfels 1995.

——, *Antwortregister*, Frankfurt/M.: Suhrkamp, 1994. – English: *Responsive Register*, trans. D. F. Goodwin (forthcoming).

——, *Deutsch-Französische Gedankengänge*, Frankfurt/M.: Suhrkamp, 1995.

——, *Topographie des Fremden*, Frankfurt/M.: Suhrkamp, 1997.

——, *Grenzen der Normalisierung*, Frankfurt/M.: Suhrkamp, 1998.

——, *Sinnesschwellen*, Frankfurt/M.: Suhrkamp, 1998.

——, "The Paradox of Expression," trans. Ch. Nagel. In F. Evans and L. Lawlor, eds., *Chiasms. Merleau-Ponty's Notion of Flesh*, Albany, NY.: State University of New York Press 2000. German: "Das Paradox des Ausdrucks." In Waldenfels 1995.

——, *Das leibliche Selbst*, ed. R. Giuliani, Frankfurt/M.: Suhrkamp, 2000.

——, "Das Phänomen des Fremden und seine Spuren in der klassischen griechischen Philosophie." In: B. Jostes, J. Trabant, eds., *Fremdes in fremden Sprachen*, München: W. Fink 2001.

——, *Verfremdung der Moderne*, Güttingen: Wallstein, 2001.

——, *Bruchlinien der Erfahrung*, Frankfurt/M.: Suhrkamp, 2002.

——, "Zwischen Sagen und Zeigen. Überlegungen zu Husserls Theorie der okkasionellen Ausdrücke." In *Studia Phaenomenologica*, Vol. III, Nos. 1–2, Bucharest: Humanitas 2003, S. 215–227. – Chinese: in *The Phenomenological and Philosophical Research in China*, Special Issue: Phenomenology in China. The Centennial of Edmund Husserl's *Logical Investigation* (2003, Shanghai) S. 125–139.

——, *Idiome des Denkens. Deutsch-Französische Gedankengänge II*, Frankfurt am Main: Suhrkamp, 2005.

Watzlawick, Paul, Beavin, Janet H., Jackson, Don D., *Pragmatics of Human Communication*, New York: W. W. Norton & Company, 1967.

Weber, Max, *Wirtschaft und Gesellschaft*, 5th ed., Tübingen: J. C. B. Mohr (P. Siebeck), 1976. – English: *Economy and Society*, trans. G. Roth and C. Wittich, Berkeley: University of California Press, 1978.

Weizenbaum, Joseph, *Computer and Human Reason: From Judgement to Calculation*, San Francisco: W. F. Freeman, 1976.

Wittgenstein, Ludwig, *Philosophical Occasions*, ed. by J. C. Klagge and A. Nortmann, Indianopolis/Cambridge: Hackett Publishing Comp., 1993.

Zahavi, Dan, *Self-Awareness and Alterity*, Evanston: Northwestern University Press, 1999.